FOREVER BECOMING

*The Ever Deepening Realization of
Presence in my Life*

VIVIAN FRANCK

Copyright © 2023 Vivian Franck.

All rights reserved. No part of this book may be reproduced, stored, or transmitted by any means—whether auditory, graphic, mechanical, or electronic—without written permission of both publisher and author, except in the case of brief excerpts used in critical articles and reviews. Unauthorized reproduction of any part of this work is illegal and is punishable by law.

Library of Congress Control Number: 2014919188

ISBN: 979-8-89031-619-6 (sc)
ISBN: 979-8-89031-620-2 (hc)
ISBN: 979-8-89031-621-9 (e)

Because of the dynamic nature of the Internet, any web addresses or links contained in this book may have changed since publication and may no longer be valid. The views expressed in this work are solely those of the author and do not necessarily reflect the views of the publisher, and the publisher hereby disclaims any responsibility for them.

Some names have been changed to protect privacy.

One Galleria Blvd., Suite 1900, Metairie, LA 70001
(504) 702-6708
1-888-421-2397

DEDICATION

*TO MY BELOVED EXTENDED FAMILY
AND MY MANY WONDERFUL FRIENDS*

ACKNOWLEDGEMENTS

Grateful Thanks

To all those dear friends who have encouraged me through the years to share my story through writing

To my editors, Kathryn Kolb, Nancy Carlson, Ivory Rieger, and Martha Fenton for their love and support throughout this whole wonderful process. I couldn't have done it without you!

To all my family and wonderful friends who were there for me when I needed them most in the hospital and nursing home: Karen, Meghan, Jenna, Linda, Arlene, Debbie, Danny, Allan, Mary Beth, Ann, Gill, Charli, Westy, Aimee, Al, Lois and Dan, Paula and Michael, Lynda, Theda, and all who dropped in to give me their love and help through it all

To my past and present dear clients, who have stuck with me through mishaps and misadventures, no matter what

To the many new friends who keep coming into my life and help expand and broaden my horizons with their fresh outlook on today's world and on life in the twenty-first century

To the many who are still with me in times of need, and celebrate with me in times of joy

Your presence during these last thirty-three years has been an inspiration, a source of strength, and a constant reminder of how loved I am

CONTENTS

Preface xi
Prologue xv

SECTION I: IS THIS FOR REAL?

Growing Up In The 30s And 40s 3
Love Wins Out 13
Loving Embrace And Major Shift 17
How Can I Live This Way? 21
A Saint's Influence In My Life 25
High School And First Attraction 31
My Love Affair With Mother Nature And Animal Friends 37
Decision Time 45

SECTION II: IS THIS REALLY, REALLY IT?

Living Up To My Promise 53
The Novitiate 55
Disappointment 59
Life As A Professed Nun 63
The Visitation 69
The Wonderful Year At The Motherhouse 77
Falling In Love 81

A Breath Of Fresh Air And Father Tom 85
The Charismatic Movement 89
Dad's Peaceful Departure 97
The Effects Of The Gifts Of The Spirit 99
Finding A Job On My Own 103
Experiencing Different Types Of Communities. 107
Emily 115
Breaking From My Original Community 119
To The New Community 123
To The Monastery. 127

SECTION III: WHAT'S REAL ANYWAY?

A New Beginning 137
Everything Falls Into Place 139
What A Zany World! 145
The Holistic Center. 151
A Long Time Wish Come True. 159
The Presence Is Everywhere 163
Learning To Drive And Buying A House 167
A Short Term Relationship 173
The Ups And Downs Of Spiritual Growth 177
God Lives In The Ever Present Moment 183
Soul Mate, Are You Out There Somewhere? 193
What Is This All About?. 199
To The Nursing Home 203
The Most Benevolent Outcome. 209

What... Again?? 213
Soul Mates Galore! 217
God's Precious Ones 219

SECTION IV: LOVE ALONE IS REAL

A Wake-Up Call 227
Abide In My Love 235
Where Am I Now? 239

Endnotes 243

PREFACE

I'd been In the convent for thirty-two years, and back in the world for a bit longer than that, when all of a sudden I felt it was time to write my life story. I'd often been encouraged by my many friends to do just that, but after a few meager attempts, my notes would always end up in the recycling bin. This was simply too difficult and exasperating a task!

In early summer of 2012, Hay House sent an invitation through the Internet inviting people to enter a book-writing contest. They were offering people a chance to win if they submitted a book by the month of October. I read about it with some interest, and then pooh-poohed it... I wouldn't even know where to begin.

A couple of weeks later, I read Anita Moorjani's book, *Dying To Be Me*, and was totally inspired by her near-death-experience which resulted in knowing herself to be a magnificent human being and unconditionally loved beyond her wildest dreams. She then was able to fearlessly engage in moving forward in her life and encouraged people to believe in their innate power to do the same. Her book proved to be the catalyst I needed to get going, and I said to myself, "Yes, I can do this!" I only had four months to write a 50,000 word memoir, and when I contacted the agent at Balboa Press, Virginia, she asked me, "Do you think you can actually do this in four months' time?" I confidently asserted, "Oh sure I can." I had absolutely no idea what writing a book entailed. Needless to say I did not win the contest, but have been adding, revising, and editing my book until now.

In the middle of September of the same year, I sustained an accident that could easily have proven fatal or reduced me to a vegetative state, but through divine intervention, it only shook me up and put me out of commission for a few days. Three or four days after this incident, I felt it was time to get together with my long-time astrologer friend, Alice Hayden, and perhaps get a clue about what was happening in my life.

During the session I mentioned that I'd entered a writing contest and had been inspired to write my memoir. She was thrilled to hear this, since my chart clearly indicated that it was time for me to write. "The times when I did your solar return before, I always told you that you had to teach," she said, "but writing is even more powerful. There are two planets in your chart that are all about writing and publishing. Communication is natural to you." She also mentioned that my capacity to get to the bottom of things, to see and remember the highlights in my life and share them, is huge. It's important for me to publish, to let my insights be known to others. "It's perfect timing for you to do this," she said.

Writing about my life has been an exercise in honesty, for I have tried to be as truthful as I can be. The story is from my perspective and will probably be viewed differently by my two living siblings. This cannot be helped, but that is quite all right with me, and I hope, with them.

It has also opened my eyes to the wonders of God's dealings with me through periods of confusion, darkness and pain, as God gently, persistently, hounded me into acknowledging and receiving the great and all-embracing reality of the Love that has always been with me and is intricately part of who I Am.

With profound gratitude and love I share my life as I recall it, seeing the mistakes, the mishaps, as well as the wonders and humor of it all, creating from moment to moment the work of art that I Am.

PROLOGUE

Gregg Braden, well-known author recognized as a pioneer in bridging science and spirituality writes in his 2008 book *The Spontaneous Healing of Belief,* "I suspect that we all experience small miracles in our lives every day. Sometimes we have the wisdom and the courage to recognize them for what they are. In the moments when we don't, that's okay as well. It seems that our miracles have a way of coming back to us again and again. And each time they do, they become a little less subtle until we can't possibly miss the message that they bring to our lives. The key is that they're everywhere and occur every day for different reasons, in response to the different needs that we may have in the moment."

These words struck such a resounding chord in my heart that I have experienced a noticeable shift in my perception and attitude towards my life story. I now see the big and small miracles that were part and parcel of my life and enabled me to grow in grace and calmness even in times of struggle and darkness through all the stages of my life.

Miracles came in many guises: my loving parent who was both father and mother to me; the gentle wise nun of my kindergarten year; the insight to stop *trying* to make friends; the wisdom to pay no attention to the talk of common illnesses of the era; realizing the necessity to forget my "little self" in order to achieve peace and joy; the daily words of help that came to me from various sources: the books I read, a word spoken by a friend or heard from a perfect stranger; the many times when eye contact with an unexpected and benign source filled me with awe and gratitude; all the times and ways that I received the *exact* answer that I needed! Then there were the bigger miracles that came after years of searching and doggedly plodding through seemingly insurmountable self-created obstacles. These are described at some length in the ensuing pages.

Gregg Braden asks that we "promise ourselves" to find at least one miracle among the many that may cross our path each day, then observe our world closely.

I have taken this homework to heart. The exercise has helped me to really take notice when something that was hard becomes easy to do: today I threaded a needle successfully on my second attempt. Unheard of for an eighty-two year-old person.

A miracle story which happened just yesterday: I came up from the basement to see my terrible-hunter-kitty, Elmer, on the hallway floor next to a dead bird. I turned around to talk with my friend who'd just come up from downstairs, then turned back to look towards the hallway to find that the bird was gone. I went looking in the different rooms asking, "Where's the bird, Elmer?" Then I heard Elmer meowing from the bedroom. I found him on top of my bureau poking into a vase of flowers there. I looked into the vase and said, "The bird's not here, Elmer. Go away." I then picked up the flowers, which needed to be discarded, and placed them in the kitchen sink. I gathered the bird feathers from the floor, then returned to the kitchen, picked up the bouquet, and went to the door.

As I opened the door, I heard some fluttering in the vase and, all of a sudden *the bird simply burst out of the flowers and flew* to the nearest tree. Alive and flying. How wonderful! I can't begin to describe all the feelings that filled my heart at the little bird's successful escape to freedom. What a perfect metaphor for the freedom that every human heart longs for and is striving to achieve. May we all be as patient and persevering as our brave little bird-friend as we continue on our own journeys.

These are small wonders, but I am grateful for them, and they simply require that I pay attention to what happens in the ever-present moment of each day to notice them. I am deeply indebted to Gregg Braden for opening my eyes to all the marvels that are still ahead for me as I continue on my journey. *Merci!*

PART ONE

IS THIS FOR REAL?

*"Let the little children come to me for theirs
is the Kingdom of God"
(Luke 2: v.1-14)*

GROWING UP IN THE 30S AND 40S

Mom and Dad were passionate lovers throughout their married life. How did we kids know this? By the way they frequently teased each other and kissed and hugged playfully in front of us, and by the fact that their bedroom door might as well have had a **"Do Not Disturb"** sign hanging from it every Sunday afternoon which produced nine children and three miscarriages over a span of seventeen years. This large a family was not an uncommon occurrence in the all-Catholic small town of Van Buren, Maine, in the 30s and 40s, and was highly applauded and encouraged by the members of the celibate clergy.

My mother and father loved all their babies to the point of being over-protective. So much so that they didn't encourage their babies to walk until they were eighteen months old. Mom worked hard to feed us, clean us, and nurse us through various kinds of illnesses throughout our childhood. I remember her singing to my little brother and me, gathering us on her lap, one on each arm, and rocking us while she sang. There was one particular little French ditty where she would insert our names, and we would ask her to sing the song over and over again. Mom would give in to our pleading and would sing until another duty called.

Once beyond early childhood, though, both Mom and Dad became overly strict and controlling with us, which, of course, they felt was their obligation. We were warned about the dangers of falling into sin even before we reached the age of reason, (seven!) and were constantly reminded not to do this or that or the other thing because it could lead to sin. We always had to watch our step to avoid going beyond any line of conduct required of good children. My parents did not intend to be mean, but they themselves were so restricted by the laws that governed their lives that they dwelt in fear of their children's smallest transgressions and so became excessively demanding and severe. Life became stifling and repressive.

When I was between the age of five and seven, I was often given special attention because I was cute and always had a smile on my face. Grown-ups, especially men, would pat me on the head and comment on how pretty I was, and I wanted to flail my arms and yell, "Leave me alone!" I was always chosen to be in parades or processions and placed up front where I could not help but be seen by everybody. I hated the attention because I was extremely shy, which nobody seemed to be aware of. Consequently, I became awfully self-conscious and started walking with rounded shoulders. My parents became concerned and consulted with the doctor who suggested that I wear a brace and do certain exercises. I remember that every evening my mother and a few of my siblings worked out with me, which made me feel loved, thus rendering the whole session more enjoyable. The experience of being singled out so early on, though, I believe, was the trigger that led me to want to learn to forget myself as a teenager. And it was also the reason why I was so afraid of being thought of as "special" when I was touched by God's grace off and on throughout my life.

When I was about two years old I developed a contemplative streak. I would ask my older sisters to pick me up and put me on the big rocking chair that stood in front of the large kitchen window so I could look outside to my heart's content. I would lose myself in the beauty before me, the undulating lawns, the many tall graceful trees that lined the street going uphill, the sound of Violet Brook gently singing among the rocks and trees below. I never spoke much, but was happy as could be just being there absorbing it all. Eventually, I became self-conscious of my behavior when one day, my mother snickered at me in front of her friend and laughingly said, "Look at that one, she could sit there all day long…" In my innocence and vulnerability, I took her remarks to mean that there was something wrong with me. As a result, I became ill at ease and I never asked to be put up on the chair again.

Thankfully, when I was in kindergarten, my nun teacher, Mother St. Claire of Mary, gave me a seat next to the window from which I had a view of the brook flowing peacefully by, the tall evergreen trees and sprawling meadow on the opposite bank, the sight of which captivated me to the point that I did not seem to be following the reading lesson. Mother would call on me to continue reading where the previous person had stopped, and then would kindly give me time to find the right place with my finger. I'd land on it and keep on reading. Mother never reprimanded me or told me to pay attention or moved me to another seat. She sweetly smiled at me, so that I never suspected anything amiss as she let me continue in my happy contemplation.

Years later, after I'd become a nun, she laughingly and gently shared this story with me. I had been totally unaware of her beneficent kindness and realized how very much her solicitous action brought something into my life that I had not even known was missing: acceptance of where I was at in the moment. No wonder I loved her so much! What a sweetheart she was—not only to me but to all the children.

At the age of three, I was given a special treat: I was chosen to go with my father to get some ice cream. My mother dressed me up in my Sunday clothes, while my brothers and sisters looked on without saying a word. I wondered at that, how come they weren't included? But I dropped the thought that something was amiss here and enjoyed the feeling of going with my father for a treat. I got into my father's truck and off we went. When he stopped the truck in front of an office building, I realized that we were not going towards the ice cream parlor at all. I started crying and strongly resisted being taken out of the truck. Dad carried me to the door yelling and crying. The door opened and a stern-faced, scary-looking man let us in. Both he and my father undressed me, put me on a table and then placed this mask of horrible smelling stuff over my nose in preparation for a tonsillectomy. I couldn't breathe, and this burning, swirling sensation of many colors was going on in my head. I thought I was going crazy. I thought "If they'd only lift the mask for a second!" But no, they didn't. Dad later said that it took all of twenty minutes for the chloroform to put me to sleep. The next thing I recall is being carried into the house by my father. He was crying and told my mother he would *never* do anything like that again. I contentedly and happily licked the ice cream cone promised me, which had come at such a price and was so richly deserved.

Some fifty years later, I attended a workshop given by a Native American healer in Portland, Maine. The workshop entailed taking some very deep breaths in a controlled way, aided by people attending the session who breathed along with the person on the table. I was on the table and doing the deep, deep breathing when suddenly an unbelievably strong smell of chloroform filled the room. People opened windows to dissipate the pungent odor and kept them open until the awful malodorous stench was gone. I realized that the chloroform had stayed in my system through all those years and was now being released from my system. Incredible! I didn't notice a distinctive difference in my body afterwards, but I'm sure getting rid of that toxic anesthetic had to be enormously beneficial in some way. What a serendipitous workshop that turned out to be.

When I was around six or seven years old, I was in a horrendous accident. Every afternoon, my father's handyman drove the pony cart back and forth to milk the cow out in the pasture. On the return home, my little brother, Ronald, had usurped the front seat where I usually sat so, I sat on the edge of the seat. We were going along smoothly when, all of a sudden, the wheels hit a rut and I flew off the seat. Instead of letting myself fall freely, I grabbed the front wheel with my right hand, rolled with it, and ended up having my head trapped under the wheel. The pony got scared and speeded up, out of control. I remember seeing the sky from my vantage point, and thinking, *"Is this how it is when you die?"* Then I blacked out. Eventually the driver was able to stop the frightened pony. The next thing I remember is standing in the back of the cart, one hand on my face, sobbing my heart out, and seeing some older girls staring at me in shock. Upon arriving home, I did not rush into my mother's arms, but into my father's protective embrace. My mother stood by, watching; I had chosen to run to my father, after all, and so she wisely let it be.

My father was the one who, with my hand gently enclosed in his, walked me to the doctor's office every day to get the bandage around my head removed and a healing salve and fresh cloth applied. I recall him squeezing my hand and gently commenting, "It must hurt, mustn't it, dear?" My heart was touched and happy tears filled my eyes.

Mom had my Dad twisted around her little finger. He was of the generation that was still chivalrous to women, and he felt he always had to be the perfect gentleman. As far as I can remember, they never quarreled, or confronted each other, but instead kept everything inside. Consequently he built resentment against Mom over the years, and when I was twelve years old and working with him at the grocery store, he started confiding in me. This did nothing to endear my mother to me. I did not ever hate my Mom. I just did not trust her.

Dad was the one who came to my piano recitals, to the spelling contests, to the school plays I was in as a high school student. I was not treated differently than any of my siblings in this way, though. My mother, for some reason, never attended any of her children's school events. A wise old psychic once told me out of the blue that my mother had once been a queen in a former life. I believed it.

I realized in my later years that my mother was also a very insecure person, which manifested as self-centeredness and overbearing ways and in never being able to admit that she was less than perfect. We could never even have a different opinion than hers. If she was contradicted in any way she would quickly resort to her favorite weapon: abundant tears, which kept flowing until the guilty party apologized profusely, begged forgiveness, and received absolution by hugging her and kissing her. Once again peace would prevail until the next opposing opinion was voiced and tears again performed their healing magic. Unfortunately, she was profoundly unaware that she was controlled by fear and anxiety.

One could always hear music playing in my home. All the popular music of the 30s and 40s emanated from our big stand-up radio in the living room throughout much of the day, and from our piano came the sometimes discordant but still delightful sounds of classical music being played by two of my older sisters. Though my father didn't play an instrument, he loved music and loved to hear his daughters play. He especially enjoyed the romantic old songs from his youth, which he would sometimes sing to my mother. Feast days, especially Christmas and New Year's, saw the whole family gathered around the piano to sing the songs of the season. We sang our hearts out, and as far as I was concerned, we were really and truly family then. I wanted these times to go on forever.

I started taking piano lessons at eight years old. I loved playing and soon was able to play little classical melodies for myself, but I was very shy and didn't like performing when people were around. I was too self-conscious about the mistakes that I could make to want an audience. To my great dismay, though, one day while practicing at the convent where I took lessons, the door to the piano room opened and a Sister stood there, listening to me play. It seems I played with great feeling, and the Sisters would pop in just to hear me perform. I was always very embarrassed whenever this happened, and would start fumbling on the keys, making all sorts of blunders. The Sisters must have realized they were making me nervous, for after a while, they stopped coming to the door to listen to me. What a relief it was not to have an audience anymore! Playing the piano was a very healing and therapeutic hobby which gave me tremendous pleasure for a good many of my growing up years.

One of the most dreaded experiences in taking lessons from the nuns as far as I was concerned, was the yearly piano recital. I remembered my older sisters talking at length about their fear and trepidation at having to memorize a piece and play it by heart in front of an audience. What if they forgot the notes they had to play? What if they made a mess of their performance? This was just too horrible to think of! They would go on for days and days, moaning and groaning about the upcoming recital while practicing like mad. The big day would arrive, and they'd inevitably come through with flying colors. Then they'd be happy pianists again until the following year when the whole scary drama would once more be reenacted.

As the time for my first piano recital drew near, I was filled with anxiety. I'd learned the lesson of worrying about performing from memory very well indeed. I had been practicing one of Mendelssohn's melodious pieces without the music in front of me for a whole month and really played it perfectly well with much feeling. Unfortunately, I listened to my fear, and when my turn came to go up on stage I asked my piano teacher if I could take my sheet music with me. She nodded in the affirmative, and so that's what I did. When I opened the piece, I looked at the notation and to my great horror did not recognize one single note! I placed my hands on the piano, and as soon as I'd begun playing I realized I'd started on the note just below the correct one. In my panic, I couldn't stop, and kept on playing one note lower than the right one to the very end. Then as though I'd not been embarrassed enough, I got up from the piano seat, turned to the audience, and smilingly genuflected to them! The audience clapped very loudly and my teacher never reprimanded me, or ever talked to me about it, which I greatly appreciated. My father, who always came to our recitals, lovingly and gently comforted me while holding my hand on our walk back home. He reassured me that I didn't have to be ashamed; that I'd do much better next year, and that I was not to worry about it. God bless his sympathetic heart.

Because of this episode I never wanted to memorize a piano piece again, and I never did. I realized at some point that I was depriving myself of great personal satisfaction and joy because of this decision, but I stubbornly refused to change my mind about it. Later, as a music teacher putting on recitals with my students, I insisted that they learn their pieces by heart, and in no way were they ever to bring their sheet music to the piano with them.

I told them that they knew their pieces very well and were capable of playing beautifully from memory. They always did just fine, and never once did any of them have any bad experience playing during a recital. In that way, I'd learned from my mistakes, and they were benefiting from them. To me, that was a fitting and very worthwhile exchange.

When I was eight years old I was scheduled to have an appendectomy at our local hospital. On the eve of the event my mother came into my room and asked, "Are you afraid?" I had not thought of being afraid, and I simply smiled. (One did not say "No" to my mother.) She took that as an affirmative and said, "If you promise God to become a nun, then everything will go all right tomorrow." I remember feeling deep resentment that she would impose this on me. Then she turned around and walked out of the room. This short encounter defined the form of my life for the next forty- two years. From that day on my mother always talked of me or introduced me as *the one who is going to become a nun.* She would never let me forget the "promise" I never made.

(Many, many years later when I asked to be released from my vows, I was required to give the reason why I wanted to take this drastic step. My answer was concise and to the point: "My mother made me promise to become a nun when I was eight years old.")

In the small Franco-American town where I grew up, it was a point of honor in large Catholic families such as mine, to have either a priest or a nun in the family. I was the designated one, I believe, because I was such a goody-two-shoes: I never made a fuss, was obedient to a fault, didn't have tantrums or become moody, and always had a smile on my face. Perfect candidate.

In later years I was able to see this episode as a blessing in disguise. I didn't particularly like being pointed out as the "nun-to-be," but that reminder along with doubts about the faith that I experienced at a very young age, probably made me seek out children's books about the saints (alongside the cowboy stories that I loved), which I found comforting and totally inspiring.

LOVE WINS OUT

Being the fifth in a family of nine children was a lot to deal with. I could not make real friends with any of my siblings. My three older siblings were much too old to associate with me. My sister three years older had a heart of gold but, did not want me in her circle of friends. My brother fifteen months younger, was an unhappy kid and did not appreciate my bouts of silliness. My sister three years younger, whom I liked and wanted to be friends with so badly, did not accept my overtures and knew exactly which buttons to push to make me cry. As for my two younger siblings, a girl and a boy, they were much too young for me to have as friends.

Thankfully, we lived in a neighborhood where there were plenty of children of all ages to play with and we frolicked enthusiastically, if at times a little roughly. I played with all the gusto and passion of a healthy little kid let loose from the strict and structured confines of a home where order and cleanliness were of the highest priority, and I hollered to my heart's content. When playtime was over, we'd often end up yelling insulting and hilarious names at each other as we parted to go back to our homes. The next day, all insults and name-calling were forgotten and forgiven as we resumed our games without reproach or bad feelings.

One of our favorite seasons was winter, which brought us loads of snow days free from school, announced by the church bell ringing at exactly 7:30 in the morning, to play and romp for as long as we could. We would create tunnels in the snow to crawl through, climb up on mountains of snow to the roof of our two-story house and jump down, have snow-ball fights, and build great big snowmen. We'd go sledding and tobogganing and skiing on the hill next door and skate on a frozen pond nearby. What tremendous fun we had! Then, when we'd had enough, we'd get the broom and sweep each other off on the porch, go back into the house with red cheeks glowing, put our jackets, pants, scarves, mittens, and hats to dry in the open oven and on radiators all over the house, and warm up with hot chocolate and snacks. We'd put everything back on as soon as the pieces of winter wear were dry and go dashing out the door for more fun! It seems we never got tired of it. As far as we were concerned winter was the absolute best! Though I recall my poor mother not enjoying it at all, and I used to wonder why she didn't like winter? What was there not to love?

It took me a while to make friends at school because the teachers had me skip the second grade. Unfortunately, the third graders I encountered were not the least bit happy to have me in their class. Who could blame them? After all, I was a whole year younger than they were; why would they want to associate with me? I was equally unhappy to be separated from my classmates and tried all sorts of ways to encourage kids to like me but, failed miserably. One of the last things I attempted was to ask my father for a candy bar from his store, then go outside and divide the bar between the girls waiting there. When this didn't work, I finally realized that trying to make friends was not the answer so, I decided to let things be. Gradually, the girls came to accept me on their own and, by the time I was in the fifth grade my friendships were solid.

Because of an overflow of children in the area, a small building had been constructed on the grounds of the big elementary school. The building was divided into two rooms which became classes for the fifth and sixth grades. We loved having classes there because rules were not observed as strictly as in the big school. The teacher, Mother Marie Louis Chanel, really liked the boys and, for what must have been reasons of her own, did not appear to like me at all. During spelling contests, we were teamed up boys against girls, and I always ended up being the last girl opposite the last boy still standing. Mother would always give me a word that had two spellings, and I knew I couldn't win, since she had decided beforehand that any word I chose to spell would be the wrong one. It never failed, and there was nothing else to do but take it in stride and accept defeat from the grinning contender who knew perfectly well what was going on.

One of the perks of being in the little school was having a longer recess period. One day, in the middle of winter and after we'd had a huge snowstorm, we kids lined up to take turns leaping off the roof of a little chicken coop on the grounds nearby. The girls ahead of me timidly hopped off from the edge of the roof. Being more daring, I thought I'd show them how to *really* jump. I started running from the back of the roof, took a flying leap, soared to the snow-covered ground below, and stayed stuck up to my waist, with my skirt (worn over my ski pants) spread out around me like a ballerina's tutu. At that moment the bell rang signaling the end of recess. "*Uh Oh,*" I thought, "*I'm in trouble!*" The boys had to shovel me out, which they enthusiastically and gleefully set to. When they were at last able to pull me up, one of my boots was left behind in the deep snow. The boy who finally brought it in to the hallway where I was standing on one foot while holding on to one of the hooks on the wall, had a grin as wide as his face and a look in his eyes that gave me a hint of how much he was enjoying the show that I had accidentally created. I walked back home to change, then returned to school to face Mother Louis Chanel's red-faced anger and strong condemning words. I felt belittled, but also felt that maybe I deserved her scolding because I'd done something that was not considered appropriate for a girl my age.

Things didn't get better between Mother Louis Chanel and me until about a year later. In those days, the children of the parish were obliged to go to church on Sunday afternoons to spend an hour or so reciting vespers (in Latin, mind you.) I was seated at the end of a pew and from my vantage point, I saw Mother Louis Chanel sit down, and observed how pale she looked. I gazed around and realized that no nun had noticed, so I got up and went to a Sister who was sitting close by and whispered in her ear, *"Mere Marie Louis Chanel est malade."* When they both walked out of church, I had a glimpse of Mother's face. She was as white as a sheet. From that day on, Mother acted very kindly and lovingly toward me, and I went through that year without any more trouble or bother.

Years later, after I'd become a nun, Mother Louis Chanel and I would meet on occasion, and she never spoke to me without tears coming to her eyes. I suspect she still regretted how hard she'd been on me, but a really beautiful relationship had built up between us from that incident, and that was all that mattered to me.

LOVING EMBRACE AND MAJOR SHIFT

Some kind of visitation happened to me that was out of the ordinary when I was about five years old. I was walking home by myself on my street one day, simply enjoying beautiful nature all around me. There was nobody else in sight. *All of a sudden I felt myself being lifted up and embraced and held close in the bosom of a Father-figure of some sort.* I had a few moments of intense joy and peace and then quickly rejected it. Who did I think I was to have such an experience? How could I speak to anybody at home about this? Nobody would believe me… or perhaps my mother would, and she'd make a big fuss about it, which I absolutely did not want. Even at that early age I knew I could not confide in my mother or anybody else. There was no way I could accept this moment of intimacy with *what I now know to be the Divine.* The following year the same thing reoccurred at about the same place. This time I refused the experience outright. I wasn't about to risk going with it; it was just too strange and unusual.

As a child I was besieged by doubts about certain aspects of the faith that we were supposed to swallow whole: babies that died without being baptized would spend eternity in limbo. Eating meat on Fridays was a mortal sin. Not going to Mass on Sunday was enough to send one to hell. I couldn't voice my doubts to anyone without being labeled a renegade, a little know-it-all who needed to be put in her place and would have been severely reprimanded by parents, teachers, priests, and everybody in town.

I often wished that the feeling of closeness with the Father that I'd experienced on my walk home would reoccur... I could've used that loving embrace once in a while. But I was not to have anything like that happen again until many years later as a young nun.

I do not remember ever having a good conversation with any of the adults in my family. We younger ones played loud and long outside but were relatively quiet inside. We played with paper dolls, board games and cards. I was pretty good at drawing, which was one of my favorite pastimes. Listening to the radio and to frightening detective serials of the time like "The Shadow Knows" was something that we kids could share and enjoy together. We'd huddle in the great big armchair next to the huge stand-up radio and hold our breath in fear and trembled in anticipation of the terrible dangers our hero was facing. We'd let out squeals of delight and relief at the inevitable, satisfactory ending, "Phew! That was a close one!" All of these activities were an escape for me.

Playing the piano was an ideal way of getting rid of all the pent-up feelings that I couldn't share with anyone. So, too, was losing myself in the imaginary world that books provided. I was an avid reader and had found a convenient place to hide to read my book especially when it was time to do dishes. I was always surprised when my family could not find me, I was hiding in plain sight really, lying down behind the footboard of my bed. I kept very quiet, and would think uncharitable thoughts about how, if they couldn't find me, that was their tough luck. Not nice at all!

I never spoke much at home, but made up for it by becoming a real loudmouth at school, subsequently always getting Ds for deportment. I often ended up having to kneel in front of the class for ten minutes or so, which I didn't mind unless the principal of the school happened to come in and witness my punishment. I would then feel myself blushing in shame, but the embarrassment and the reprimand over, I kept on talking anyway. I didn't care. My grades were good, I had plenty of friends, and the penalty wasn't really all that bad.

I ended up paying for my loquaciousness during my freshman year in high school. The student body was gathered in the school auditorium to receive report cards from the principal of the school, a strict and imposing nun. She was seated on the stage, and when called we all went up, one by one, to receive our cards. It so happened that every girl in my class had a bad grade for deportment. I went up when my turn came, and when Mother pointed out that I also had a D, I unfortunately smiled. My habit of smiling to hide any emotions really worked to my disadvantage that time! Mother was infuriated. She got dangerously incensed and yelled, "YOU DARE TO SMILE?" and went on and on and on, then refused to give me my report card. Thoroughly abashed and humiliated, I turned around with flaming face and walked down the few steps to sit in my place until we were dismissed. Thankfully, one of my teachers came over and kindly handed me my card as I later went sobbing out the door. I made my way to church where I could sit anonymously and finish crying before I headed home. My face was a mess; my mother commented on it, and asked me about it, but I refused to open up to her. I probably missed an opportunity to change my attitude a little towards my mother then, but the outcome was too uncertain and I was not willing to give her the benefit of the doubt.

A major shift in my understanding of health and sickness occurred when I was eleven years old. There was a lot of talk going around about all the major illnesses of the day. Diphtheria was a common subject of conversation, tuberculosis was another, as was infantile paralysis. I realized that if I kept on listening to all this negative talk, I would eventually let fear take over and make myself ill, so I decided to turn my thoughts to something else while my friends spoke about this one and that one getting sick, and how awful it was, and so on. It was difficult to stick to my decision because part of me was curious and wanted to listen, but an inner wisdom prevailed, and I have lived my life like that ever since.

I have never paid attention to ads talking about various diseases and the medicines to cure them, nor do I ever look up what symptoms can be a sign of disease. I have always believed that focusing on staying healthy rather than talking about illnesses that can happen is a much better way to live. I realize now that grace was certainly with me when I made that shift as a young girl, and I can only be humbly grateful for the inspiration that has served me so well.

If my physical well-being was pretty much in my control, and I had no anxiety that way, my emotional and spiritual well-being was another story.

HOW CAN I LIVE THIS WAY?

We were an overtly religious family. Every evening after supper, we all convened in the living room to pray the rosary. No one was ever excused. The older siblings as well as the younger ones knelt through the long, seemingly endless repetition of the Hail Marys, followed by the recitation of the litanies of the saints. I remember spending the time making up a story about the western movies we saw on Saturdays and created one episode after another every evening. Of course, I was always the heroine. That made the long prayers bearable, anyway.

Lent was a time of being deadly earnest about penance and none of us ate any candy for six weeks. We all traipsed off to church for the 6 a.m. Mass, no matter the weather. If the car wouldn't start because of 40-degrees-below-zero weather, we'd walk. And there were the extra church things to do, such as the stations of the Cross every Friday, and more fish days than ever. All of this was done religiously, no exceptions. No wonder we couldn't wait for the six weeks to be over and Easter was such a treat with its gaily decorated Easter baskets full of goodies hidden all over the house. The joys of the Lenten period being over for a whole year!

But, as with most Catholic families in our area, our religion was practiced with fear and apprehension. By the time I was seven, it was time for First Confession in preparation for First Communion. The nun prepared us by reading a long list of possible sins. Being the sensitive and fearful little Virgo I was, I took everything to heart and worried about whether or not I had committed some of these sins. Needless to say, *I hated confession with a passion that never left me,* so much so that it was the first religious practice I discontinued as soon as I left the convent. The whole school was walked off to church to go to confession every three weeks. And as though the nuns' and the priests' moralizing was not enough, our parents were so fearful that we would do something wrong, like become pregnant, that they went overboard teaching us about the possible ways that we could fall into sin. Looking at pictures in magazines, accidentally seeing my little brother pee, listening to and singing the words of certain songs, could all lead to mortal sin. My very thoughts could be dangerous and lead me astray. There was no safe place, no safe way to be in this world. I felt so restricted and boxed in that I remember thinking, *Is this the way God is? How can I live this way?*

Was God really going to sentence someone to eternal damnation for all these supposed failings? I could not believe it, yet I dared not voice my doubts and questions to anyone. I trudged along as best I could, living in the hope that someday things would change for the better. I kept as quiet and unobtrusive as possible and became very adept at repressing my true feelings, thoughts, imagination, and gifts; a skill I did not understand was so harmful to me.

It also seemed like everybody in town kept an austere eye out for wayward young teenagers. I remember someone calling my mother to tell her that my dear sister, Charlotte, three years older than I, had been seen talking with a boy on the street. And of course, my sister was given a very forceful reprimand by both my parents. Sure, she was boy-crazy, but that was no reason to restrict her so severely. This just served to harden her in her determination to leave home just as soon as she could. Sadly, she left convinced that she was the black sheep of the family, being the only one who had dared defy my father. She had a pretty miserable life and died at the early age of sixty-one.

A SAINT'S INFLUENCE IN MY LIFE

Around fourteen years of age, I began pondering whether I really wanted to be a nun or not. I still played with friends, went to the movies, read books about the wild west and mystery stories, but I also read the lives of the saints. One particular saint's story really inspired me, and I read her autobiography at least once a year, trying to absorb her wonderful spirit. She is St. Therese of the Child Jesus, (also known as Therese of Lisieux) a Carmelite nun who entered a contemplative Community at the age of sixteen, lived a life of unconditional love, and took upon herself the mission of embodying in her short life total trust and unflinching confidence in God, her Father. She lived in an era where Jansenism was vogue in the Catholic Church, promoted by a priest who preached fervently and intensely about hell-fire and damnation for the least infraction of the ten commandments as well as the smallest violation of rules and regulations among members of religious communities. Jansenism was later recognized as a heresy by the Church.

Therese did not place any credence to this deviation, but continued to put her trust in a loving God, and instilled in the young novices under her care, a deep and lasting belief in His undying Love for all. She so inspired the other nuns in the Community (as well as her own blood sisters, who were also Carmelite nuns) that one of them, the eldest and the Mother Prioress at the time, was moved to write Therese's life story, *L'Histoire d'une Ame*, when Therese lay dying of tuberculosis at the young age of twenty-four. She became known as the Saint of The Little Way, because she followed Jesus' teaching to become like little children. That is, she lived her life without fear and trusted in a loving Father to take care of her every need even when, towards the end of her life, she lost her faith in God. She lovingly accepted this painful experience simply for what it was—a trial. Most saints experience what has been called the "dark night of the soul," which is a period of spiritual desolation suffered by a spiritual seeker in which all sense of consolation is removed, and one feels profoundly alone. It seems to be a necessary part of the commitment to spiritual growth.

I definitely wanted to emulate St.Therese. So, at the age of fourteen, I made the decision that when the time came I would take the necessary steps to attempt to enter a Carmelite Community. I remember being disappointed when I didn't die at the age of twenty-four like the little saint. In the meantime I tried to be as loving as possible towards everybody, as Therese had been.

My oldest sister, Velma, who had MS, had a fiery temper and was very difficult to live with. To get as much exercise as she could she'd insist on walking to church for Mass every morning. I took on the responsibility of helping her go wherever she wanted to go. Physically helping her was the easy part; having to listen to her ranting and raving about one member of the family or another was grueling. I listened, let her talk, and gave as little attention to what she said as possible. I knew in some way that she was not responsible for her anger, and so I hung in there.

Years later as a nun, I came to be with her at the end of her life. During Velma's last six months of life, she was put into a nursing home. This was because our mother could no longer take care of her. On the eve of Velma's death, I sat with her through the night accompanied by a Sister who had often attended dying people. I'd never seen anyone die before, so Sister's kindness and focused attention in ministering to Velma was a valuable education for me. Before taking her last breath, Velma looked at me with shining eyes full of love and gratitude and gave me the most radiant smile I'd ever seen. Around five o'clock in the morning, my forty-one year old sister joyfully and peacefully went home to God.

A few years later, I dreamed of her. She was in heaven, I believe, not only standing up but dancing! With arms spread wide open, she showed off her lovely dress, and smiled glowingly and radiantly at me while twirling around in unbounded happiness. I knew this was the *real* Velma. The angry, bitter personality she'd carried around all her life had only been a caricature of her true nature and essence. What a lesson this was for me.

At the same time, I imitated St. Therese in a way she would not have approved. She had gone through a period of scrupulosity, so I was going to become scrupulous. I had that tendency anyway, with my exaggerated fear of sinning, of doing the wrong thing. I purposely and very unwisely took steps in that direction, which meant that I'd look back and examine every action, every thought that came my way. Talk about self-sabotage! Consequently I became stuck in a state of great confusion and fear for many years.

I now realize that in a very unconscious way I was believing my own thoughts: *"I should do this to become like Therese."* This was utter nonsense! But I did not comprehend this until many years later.

By the age of sixteen I had worked myself into a miserable condition. During this time I read a story in a Reader's Digest of a young girl in some island country who'd been possessed by the devil. One night, on the verge of going to sleep, the story hit me hard and I was filled with fear. I couldn't sleep for the longest time. In the morning, I woke up crying, and my father came to console me. It was decided that I would make an appointment to talk to a priest I knew that very day.

In the small town where I grew up counseling was not available. Whenever anything worrisome came up, one could go talk to a favorite priest, who, in this instance, was gentle Father Paul. He was kind, and much less rigid in his thinking and preaching than the other priests. He listened to my story and to my fear and told me that he thought I was psychic. I had no idea what the word meant, so I thought I was going through some psychological thing or other, which increased my fear. At home, I found the definition of psychic in the dictionary and gradually stopped worrying about it.

Fear of things psychological came from my mother, who had the bad habit of spilling out her fears on any one of us nine children who chanced to be around, at any given moment. She obviously didn't realize that some of us would be affected by her fears because we were so young. Before menopause she became very fearful of going crazy because she'd heard that women could become mentally ill during that period in their lives. It so happened that I was often nearby when she started voicing her distress. I was just a little child and would stand transfixed, not able to move, wanting her to stop, feeling her anguish. Then I'd run outdoors and play, play, play until I got rid of the fear. My mother never went crazy, but I coped with the anxiety about mental illness off and on for years.

When I got older and talked of the fear that would come up periodically to a couple of wise and knowledgeable friends, I was reassured that I was fine mentally. I also learned to simply say to God, "Hey! If you want that for me, I accept it!" I'd put him in charge of my mental health as well as my physical well-being, entrusting myself to His great Love, and just stopped worrying. That worked for me.

I also realize that I was *ashamed* of being fearful, just as I was *ashamed* of feeling anger, which made it impossible for me to speak about these feelings to anyone for the longest time. I know better now, thank God. There's nothing shameful about having feelings. It's part of being human, and one simply needs to deal with them as they show up.

HIGH SCHOOL AND FIRST ATTRACTION

A few years ago, at a high school reunion, and as a person back in the world, one of my former classmates told me that when he and some other boys would approach me as I talked openly and freely with my girlfriends, I'd clam up the minute they appeared. They actually felt a wall come down in front of them. High voltage! Don't come too close. My not available radar was working full time. Surprisingly, though, I was allowed to go to the high school dances once a month, and I enjoyed dancing tremendously. That was acceptable to me for it did not present a problem to my envisioned vocation since the boys I could have been interested in never asked me to dance, and in those days, it was not suitable for girls to ask boys to be their partners.

Of course, I had crushes on boys throughout my high school years, hoping to come across a selected one on the sly, but not pushing myself on anyone or making any kind of advances at all. I tried to imagine what it would be like to have a boyfriend, and looked at my girlfriends who were dating with a little envy.

The prospect, though appealing, never got any further than having blissful dreams of going out with somebody. This was okay with me. It was less scary to create fantasies from afar than to actively engage in a relationship. I just did not trust myself. I could behave foolishly and live to regret it; I was not about to take that chance.

I was also part of a group of boys and girls who went to the movies together, went for ice cream after the show, hung out to play in the snow, skied and skated and went tobogganing. It was tremendous fun and we enjoyed ourselves thoroughly, and to my way of thinking it was absolutely non-threatening. Plus combined boys and girls high schools put on a play every year directed by the priests who taught at the boys' school. I absolutely loved to be on stage (my Leo rising sign showing here) and was really a good actress, so I was always part of every play, to my great delight. This provided another opportunity to laugh and be silly and relish the whole experience of boy-girl camaraderie that would not have been available otherwise. I felt that all of these activities provided some degree of normality to my life. Life was pretty good.

As a high school senior, I was asked to go to the prom by a classmate. One of my sisters, Charlotte, three years my senior, answered the phone and took it upon herself to give a categorical, "No, she can't go to the prom." I happened to be close by and overheard her, but, as was my wont, smilingly accepted my fate without a complaint, even though I was surprised by my sibling speaking for me and sort of resented it. I had totally bought in to the very Catholic idea that if I went through any kind of suffering it meant that God loved me. Sad to say, I believed this gross distortion of the truth for a good part of my life as a nun.

When World War II started, my oldest brother, Jimmy, who'd been working with my father at his store, joined the Marines. When he left, Dad asked which one of us would be interested in working with him. I jumped at the chance and offered to take Jimmy's place. I hated housework and adored my father. What a break. So at age eleven, I worked after school until closing time at 6pm, then all day Saturday, from 6am to 11pm. I worked all through the summer, with a short one-week vacation to go to my grandparents' camp on the lake and have some fun. This regime continued until I turned eighteen years old.

I was happy working at my father's store. He and I had a close and comfortable relationship often filled with spirited laughter in spite of the hard physical labor. I remember the wonderful smile he always gave me, and when I needed to feel God's love for me, I always envisioned the love in my father's eyes. I think that is why I have always found it easy and comfortable to relate to God as "Father."

I believe that my father embodied more of the feminine principle than my mother. He was very kind, thoughtful and generous toward us and toward people in need. I remember a huge stack of unpaid bills that had built up over the years, sitting on the counter at the store. Most of these had accrued during the years of the depression when my Dad simply could not refuse food to the families who had no means of paying for it. He never expected to be repaid, but every once in a while someone would come in, introduce himself, and pay an old bill that was probably twenty-five years old. Dad would fill up with tears when this occurred. He felt very "God-like" to me.

Working at the store was physically very hard and demanding. I'm sure Dad did not realize (neither did I) that carrying heavy boxes of canned goods from the basement up to the first floor took quite a toll on my young body, as did having the huge front-carrying basket on my bike laden with loads of food. In those days no one really knew the way to bend and lift to lessen the strain on one's back muscles and prevent sometimes lasting injury to the back and to delicate inner organs. I worked with back pain most of the time, without complaint: I figured everybody had pain, so why even mention it? I eventually found out I had sciatica, and possibly all my female problems dated from that time, too. We just didn't know any better, did we? Everything was just accepted as part of life, and we simply did what needed to be done.

Some time during my teen years, an interesting foreshadowing of future events happened. My father was not feeling well and had gone to lie down on his bed. Mom always saw to all my father's needs, but this time, as I came into the room to see him, he asked me to give him a back rub. I'd never done anything like that before, so I cautiously climbed onto the bed, straddled him and went to work. When I was done, he turned around, looked at me and exclaimed, "My, but you have good hands!" I was pleased, but I thought, "I'll never be able to make a living doing this." Little did I know that years later, I would be eating my words and using my hands to help relieve people's muscular aches and pains and even getting paid for doing so.

I graduated at age sixteen. After graduation, I had a week off and spent it with one of my sisters who was working for a family in a different town. One of the boys from that household, Billy, took a liking to me and I took a liking to him. He was the kind of boy that any girl would dream of: good- looking, neat, polite, considerate and fun. We were never alone together, so there was no risk involved there. We simply enjoyed talking and laughing and spent all the time we could together. After I returned home and resumed working at the store, Billy sent his younger brother over to my town and to the store to do some reconnoitering; I guess he wanted to find out what I looked like in my own setting. It so happened that I was doing some clean-up job at the time, my hair hidden under a kerchief and my appearance quite soiled: I was anything but attractive. I smiled at Tommy and talked a bit with him, but never apologized for how I looked. He was sweet and polite, but did not stay around for very long. I never saw or heard from Billy again, and though I was a little sad, I got over it quickly enough. Still, I never forgot him, and sometimes wondered what life would have been like if I had allowed that relationship to blossom. Realistically speaking, it could never have evolved past the friendship stage because of our very different backgrounds and social status. Billy was a lovely being, but I would never have been accepted by his family, and my parents would most certainly have strongly refused the alliance. It would have been doomed from the outset. I did not make a big deal of it, and so life went on as before, for yet a little while.

A significant workshop that I experienced as a nun many years later opened my eyes about the kind of relationship I'd had with my parents from a very early age. The teacher, Jackie, had invited laymen, priests and nuns to participate in a fifteen-week course on interpersonal relationships. Jackie was a stern, dedicated, Irish Catholic who'd studied in the Far East, educating herself in the mystical spirituality of that area. She gave us maxims to absorb that were extremely useful. For instance: "No label, Mabel," "Don't sweat the small stuff," "Swing and sway with the Lord today," "Hi, God!" (to everything we saw), "No mind" (stop thinking so much), "Fine, double fine" (nothing can faze us). All really helpful to use as mantras.

She would give us homework each week and would ask us to report on it the following week. One week our homework was to make two columns, one titled *Father,* the other titled *Mother.* We copied the fifty attributes that she'd written on the board and were told to specify which ones belonged to whom. The following week, she asked for a volunteer to go up to the board and indicate in which column the character traits belonged. In keeping with who I am, I volunteered. I went up, and as she pointed to the different characteristics, I said, mother... father... mother... father... all the way down the rows. When I was done she placed her hands on her hips and yelled: "WHEN ARE YOU GOING TO STOP LIVING YOUR MOTHER'S AND FATHER'S LIVES AND START LIVING YOUR *OWN* LIFE?" I was stunned and speechless, for I had not expected such an adverse response to my openness and willingness to share. Plus the teacher did not offer any further help. What could I do with this information? Where to start? How to go about it?

At some point I realized I often thought and behaved like my parents and rarely followed my own inner wisdom. So little by little, through the years, as l caught myself mirroring their behavior, I learned to laugh a little at what I was doing, stop, let it go, and move on. So far this has worked fine for me.

MY LOVE AFFAIR WITH MOTHER NATURE AND ANIMAL FRIENDS

For as long as I can remember, I've had a love affair with Mother Nature. My father, who had been a game warden for the first ten years of his marriage, knew the woods of northern Maine like the back of his hand. Every Sunday, from the time that I was very small, the family would go on outings in the woods. We would never go to the same place twice, and Dad would always find a delightful nook where we could stop and have our picnic lunch and enjoy beautiful nature around us. I remember once coming to a clearing surrounded by tall pines, where the fallen needles provided a soft gentle carpet for us as we sat down and leaned against the trunks of trees for back support. The sun was streaming through the circle of trees that day and shining full blast on this space; everything was shimmering with a gorgeous golden aura. It was breathtakingly enchanting! We sat down, silently munching our food, not wanting to spoil the deep peace and contentment that surrounded us and filled us.

After lunch Dad would conduct a little nature class: he'd lead us through paths in the woods while pointing out details of the multi-colored leaves, and giving names to the trees and bushes with fruit clinging to them. He showed us which berries were edible and which were poisonous, which plants to be wary of touching (the shiny three leaves of poison ivy) and which ones we could handle without fear. He was a great teacher, and I loved him for it. Our next favorite thing to do was to lie down, look up at the sky to see what pictures we could make of the fluffy white clouds passing by and make up stories about them. After a couple of hours or so, Dad would give us the word: time to pack up and drive back home! We'd scurry along picking up empty bags and left-overs, clamber up into the back of the truck, and lie down with a collective sigh, well relaxed, refreshed and contented. What a glorious day was Sunday; after church, that is.

I did not realize it then, but I now know that this time of communing with nature was just as sacred as going to church, if not more so. The bonding that we felt with each other as a family on those days was truly special, since it was one of the times when harmony and genuine love for each other prevailed; the other times being the holidays and each other's birthdays. Generally speaking, as far as I was concerned, I felt we were not a very close family, so anything that brought us together was really appreciated and treasured by me. I have to say that with the passing of years, communicating with my only two living siblings has become better, though still guarded.

Later, when times were very tough and potato farming became a thing of the past, Dad, who had always loved farmers and their farms, would spend Sunday afternoons going berry picking on the abandoned farms. He felt badly that all this abundance was going to waste. I was always the one who volunteered to go picking with him for it truly was a delicious adventure and it was so satisfying to bring those luscious berries home for everyone to enjoy.

To this day, I spend as much time as I can outside, whether to walk the hills around my home, to sit down and enjoy the lovely garden in my backyard, or sit on a bench on the Eastern Prom in Portland to enjoy the awesome view of Casco Bay and its islands extending out to the horizon. Once last summer, I was walking along reveling in the beauty of God's creation, when out of the blue, I heard the words "I AM" coming from the trees, the grass, the flowers around, the very road I was walking on… and I marveled at God's Presence manifesting as everything around me. Mother Nature makes me happy.

As for loving animals: that's what got me the name of "Cry-Baby." I'd be sitting down in the living room's big stuffed chair, reading *Bambi* or *Lassie Come Home*, or some other animal story, and cry my eyes out. Inevitably, my big brother would hear my sobs from wherever he was, come in the room to witness my tears, and yell out, "CRY BABY!" over and over again. I didn't stop crying, of course; I just cried more. We always had a cat and sometimes a dog and I always felt badly when they were not treated with love and kindness, though I never dared express my true feelings to the family. I chose to be the caretaker of the animals we had whenever that was possible, making up for what I considered to be the callousness of my siblings and sometimes of my father, by pouring out all my affection on them.

Years later, when visiting my mother at the Nursing Home in our hometown one day, I spoke to her of my wonderful relationship with my kitty, Misty, the first cat I ever called my own. She surprised me by saying: "I never knew you liked cats." And I thought, Dear Mom, there were lots of things you didn't know about me. But I never shared that thought; I didn't want to open a pandora's box.

My father had a real inferiority complex about his French-Canadian background. I was always saddened by the fact that he always kow-towed to English speaking people. When I was twelve years old, I had charge of my brother Jimmy's dog, Sandy, while he was in the service. One day a man (clearly English-speaking) stopped by the store, looked at Sandy, liked him, and asked Dad if he could have him. I was stunned when my father said, "Sure!" *I couldn't believe that this was actually going to happen!* How could my father do this to me and to Sandy? And of course, I never dared confront him about it.

Sure enough, the following Sunday, the man drove up to our house to pick up Sandy. I was the one who was expected to lead him into the car, because he would surely follow me. He did. I went in through one door and out the opposite door, and a boy closed the door on him. I gazed at the receding vehicle and *I knew then that hearts could break*. Mine was hurting so much! I looked up towards the house. The rest of my family was on the porch, silently watching the transaction take place. Without a word, I walked by them and went up to my room. I resolved then and there that I would *never* let myself become so strongly attached to anything or anyone again, and that I would *never, ever* cry again. I went down to supper as I was expected to, ate with a heavy heart in the midst of deafening silence, then went off by myself to some corner of the house to grieve.

I never cried when both my grandparents died or at any other death. I just knew they were happier in heaven anyway. I forgave my Dad, for way down deep he was really a very kind and gentle man. He was just misguided, that's all.

A relatively happy ending: About a year after Sandy was taken away from me, a car parked across the street from Dad's store... the door opened, and Sandy came running out! I was out like a flash and in seconds Sandy and I were all over each other in the middle of the street—empty at that time of day.

After lots of hugs and kisses, we separated; Sandy returned to the car and I went back into the store filled with joy and peace and gratitude, for I knew then that Sandy was with a family that took good care of him.

Once I was out of the convent and on my own, I ventured to get a little kitty after about four years of apartment living. Misty was a sweetheart, a big beautiful grey part Maine Coon cat. He was two months old when he came into my home and heart. What a delight to have this frisky bundle of joy running throughout the rooms! He would follow me around, never leaving my side. Once, while I was simply standing, I felt a tugging on my bathrobe. I looked down and there was Misty climbing up my robe! With a laugh, I grabbed my camera, never far away after Misty came into my life, and took a photo of him striving to scramble up my body. He was truly adorable and a real lap-cat. The minute I sat down, there came Misty. I couldn't imagine being without him, but regrettably he was with me for only eight years. Being an indoor-outdoor cat, he developed some kind of disease in his mouth that the vet didn't recognize. I had limited resources and could not afford the tests that would have been necessary to diagnose his problem, so it became necessary to have Misty put to sleep.

I sorrowfully and tearfully held him in my arms for the final injection, and actually felt his spirit leave his body and wrap itself around my neck, which made me cry even harder. At some point while I was driving home, I realized that this was the first time I cried over a death since I'd hardened my heart so long ago. Misty had effected a healing within me, bless his dear little cat-heart. Pets are such healers and gifts to us humans. The nuns, who were not allowed to have an animal because having an attachment to anything was against the rules, did not know what they were missing.

I felt his cat presence with me for about a week, then told him he could leave. I vowed that I would never get another cat (famous last words). Losing Misty was just too painful an experience.

It was a few years before I ventured to get another cat from the animal shelter. Lucky was a beautiful, sleek, black cat, as sweet as they come, but he was with me for only four months when he was hit by a car right in front of my house. It seems the driver was one who had a vendetta against black animals in the neighborhood. Thank God, he left the area soon after this episode, for after being without an animal for a couple of years I took in two black cats, Mickey and Coney, who lived and thrived for fifteen and seventeen years respectively.

I loved them dearly but they were quite a challenge being both outdoor cats and genuinely big hunters! I didn't mind when they brought in dead mice, but bringing them in *live* was quite another story. Probably the funniest episode happened when I was sitting in bed reading one evening. By that time I suspected that there were live mice in the house, since I was not always able to catch them by the tail and send them flying to their freedom. Anyway, I noticed something in my peripheral vision and looked around and saw this cute little mouse sniffing at the lovely-smelling foot salve I had in a tin box. I quietly got up, went to get my rubber gloves in the kitchen, came back and stood above my little friend, waiting for a chance to grab his tail. I lunged… and missed! It flung itself onto the bedpost, four legs holding on to the post, and looked up straight at me. My God, but it was cute! I didn't move, and it returned to that wonderful-smelling stuff on the bed-side table. This time, I had to grab his tail with my left hand, and I got it! It was furious! It twisted around and bit me, but never pierced my rubber glove. I quickly went to the door and flung it out. I saw it shaking its little body a bit as it landed, then watched it disappear into the long grass. I eventually locked the in-coming cat door until my two lovely cats learned that if they wanted *in*, they had to keep the mice *out*. They did and we lived happily ever after.

After Mickey and Coney were gone, I was graced with a wonderful tiger cat named Elmer who is almost human in his understanding of my needs. He's comforted me more than once when I got physically hurt, rubbing his head against mine and purring soothingly. But, he's also a big hunter and has given me some bad moments, such as the time he brought in a live crow, which thankfully, I was able to save. All in all he meows to me when I talk to him, "talks" in his sleep, follows me on my walks, plays too roughly, but still gives me much joy.

Cats are amazing teachers of patience; they never bear grudges and are always forgiving, and they are tremendous models for living in the present moment of Now.

DECISION TIME

As far as going away to enter a community, I knew it was up to me to make a move. I had done some preliminary investigating. I'd written to a few Carmelite Orders and asked if I could be received in their Community. The Carmelites are a strict contemplative order and go through a long discernment process for each applicant that contacts them. After reading about why I wanted to join them and asking about God's will for me, each Community sent me a negative reply. I was disappointed, but also felt some relief, and was actually glad not to be chosen. Such a strict and structured life was a little much, even for my bizarre taste for suffering.

Now I had to find a Community that I wanted to join. Any Community but the Community that had taught me in school would be acceptable.

The schools in my town, even though they were public, had nuns in charge. It seems that in the early 1900s a town magistrate walked all the way to the state capitol, hundreds of miles away, to plead the case for bringing in a religious community to teach in the schools, since all the town was Catholic. He won. Soon the nuns became the primary educators, though there were always some lay teachers in every school.

Most of the nuns in the elementary schools were okay. But I felt that some of the high school teachers were biased against me. This trait revealed itself especially when my father got permission from the mayor to take me out of school in the morning for a month to help him out at the store. I was a freshman at the time and missed all the school subjects that were taught in the a.m. The nuns never offered to fill me in on what I'd missed; and I never dared to ask for help because I felt the Sisters who would have to find time outside the regular school hours to help me would not be happy about it, and so I coped as best I could. I lost all interest in school. From consistently having an A on my report card I went to being a C and D student. Not until my senior year did a teacher, Mother Mary Laura, take enough of an interest in me to help me and encourage me to work harder in my classes. Because the nuns had been so disinterested in my welfare I just could not picture myself being part of that particular Community, but of course, that's exactly the Community I joined! Here is how it happened:

A classmate of mine was leaving for Boston to begin studies in a nursing program at Carney Hospital. After I heard about what Molly was going to do, I contacted her and made arrangements, unbeknownst to my parents, to join her on her journey. I had made enough money to be able to pay for my fare and a room in a hotel. When the arrangements were made, I told my parents that I was going on vacation for a week and that I was also going to meet with Father Paul, the priest who had been my mentor a couple of years earlier. My father was not happy! He did not want me to go, for whatever reason he didn't tell me, and I didn't want to know. He probably was scared for me: I was a small town girl who'd never been away from home on my own, venturing out into the vast unknown of the big city of Boston, Massachusetts. I did have a great deal of trepidation about the trip but wasn't about to show it.

On the morning that I left with Molly, my father had not changed his attitude, and wounded me to the quick when he refused to give me a hug and a kiss goodbye. I was determined to go and was not going to change my mind. There was no future for me working in my father's store, and no future in remaining in my lovely but provincial hometown. This was the first of many "now or never" decisions that I would eventually make throughout my life.

Once in Boston my friend went off to Carney School of Nursing, and I was left to fend for myself in the big city. Molly had directed me to a boarding house where I spent the night, tossing and turning with the rumbling of nearby trains and the clanging noises and roar of cars keeping me awake. Who would ever want to live in this city day after day after day, I thought. The next morning I asked the lady of the house for directions to a breakfast place. She mumbled directions, and I was too embarrassed to say that I had not understood a word she'd said, so I paid her for the night's lodging and took off. I figured I would come across a diner *somewhere* in a city this size.

I soon realized I was in a business district, but I kept on walking in the hope that something would turn up. I spied a big Coca-Cola sign not too far off, and thought I'd at least get myself a coke to drink. I opened the big door, walked in and saw only big machines around, nothing that looked like a soda fountain at all. Three men looked at me in astonishment, and wearing a great big grin on his face, one of them came forward and asked me what he could do for me. I knew something was wrong here, but I stoutly asked him, "I'd like a coke-float, please." His grin got inches wider and he explained that only coke machines were sold in this particular store. He kindly pointed to a place within walking distance where I could get something to eat. Sheepishly I turned around, blushing like crazy, and as I opened the door he asked, "Where do you come from?" And I knew I shouldn't have answered, but I said loud and clear, "Maine!" . . . then left, almost running out of the place. I did find somewhere to eat and also experienced how easy it would be to get picked up. This was 1949, a few short years after the end of the war, and there were plenty of doughboys home on furlough. One soldier, young and very handsome, eyed me and smiled encouragingly at me. I was apprehensive, and pointedly avoided looking at him, paid for my doughnut and coke at the checkout, and went out of that diner as fast as I could. A big city could be frightening!

Later that morning I met with Father Paul. He was very kind and considerate as usual, and tried to pin down exactly what I was looking for in a religious community. He suggested a Missionary Order. "Nope. Not for me." "A Nursing Order?" "No." "A Teaching Order?" "Maybe—I think I would like to teach, but not with the Community that taught me." He named several teaching orders that I could look into, and I said I would do just that, (which, of course, I didn't do) and left to go back to the safety of the boarding house where I spent another night listening to screeching engines, wailing sirens, and creaking sounds until dawn finally broke through.

The following day I went to Lawrence MA, north of Boston, to visit with Mother Mary Laura, the helpful teacher I'd loved as a senior in high school. As we talked, she asked, "Vivian, would you like to teach?" "Yes," I replied, "I think I would." "Well," she said, "The Community received new novices for training a few days ago. Would you be interested in finding out if you would be accepted at this late date?" I hesitated, took the plunge and said, "Yes, I would." Because of an inherent timidity I failed to mention that there was a "but": I positively *did not want to teach piano*. Still I did not back off, even though I had butterflies cavorting in my stomach and plenty of misgivings about what I was about to do.

Mother Mary Laura then phoned the head of the Community, Mother Mary Leah, known as the Provincial Superior, talked with her about my situation, then returned to the parlor to see me. The Provincial had said she would receive me on the following day and talk with me about my vocation. She knew of me, since I'd been taught by her nuns from early childhood, and she was a second cousin of mine, though I'd never known her personally. The next day, accompanied by two sisters, I ignored my nervousness and my "what ifs?" and took off for the Provincial House in southern Maine, about two hours away.

And so began the second part of my life. I was on my way, but to what? I didn't know. I simply blindly trusted that I was making a move in the right direction.

PART TWO

IS THIS REALLY, REALLY IT?

*"This is my commandment:
love one another, as I have loved you."
(John15:v.10)*

LIVING UP TO MY PROMISE

When a girl entered the convent, she was expected to bring a trousseau along, that is, certain articles of clothing such as black stockings, a couple of petticoats made to order, certain pieces of underwear, etc. I had none of these articles, so was given clothes that more or less fit me. The veil, the dress, everything about the outfit was homely and ugly; but, I was going to have to live with it, since this was my choice, after all.

One thing I'd completely forgotten to do was to let my parents know about these last-minute developments. I was supposed to arrive by train in my hometown the following day. Monday morning came, and no Vivian. I have no idea what went through their minds at this point. They never brought it up, and I never asked. All they got was a card from me on the Tuesday, telling them that I'd entered the convent. Somehow, in my nervousness, I'd forgotten there was such a thing as a telephone, because I didn't even *think* of calling them.

Needless to say, the whole family was overjoyed. So much so, that a couple of weeks later I got a surprise visit from Mom, Dad, and my oldest sister, Velma. My Dad jumped from his chair when he saw me, caught me in a bear hug, and couldn't stop crying and laughing at the same time. He begged my forgiveness for his behavior of a few weeks earlier. Of course I forgave him. And my relationship with Mom, though always superficial, was much more cordial after I entered the convent. I'm sure she was very relieved that I was finally *living up to my promise*, and that at last there was going to be a nun in the family.

THE NOVITIATE

I went through the required two years of training in the Community of the Sisters Servants of the Immaculate Heart of Mary, better known as The Good Shepherd Sisters of Quebec, so named because it was founded to do the works of the Good Shepherd: taking in women who, when coming out of prison, had no place to go. Gradually, the Community grew and expanded to include a home for unwed mothers; a place for juvenile delinquents; the women's prison in Quebec; the Creche St. Vincent de Paul, where there were always about eight hundred babies waiting to be adopted; and finally, schools throughout the entire province of Quebec and in Maine and Massachusetts.

The novitiate (the word "novitiate" is used to denote both the physical building we lived in and the training we received) was a two year program of study and reflection; a time to discern whether or not we were really called to be nuns. The building was a former hotel and sat on a lovely lawn that had a walkway bordered by yellow, red, and purple pansies smiling at us as we made our way from the large porch to the Atlantic Ocean almost at our doorstep. We were not allowed to go into the magnificent Atlantic, but were encouraged to stride along the boardwalk in our heavy serge habits and pray for the poor sinners in their skimpy bathing suits.

The training for us postulants was somewhat eclipsed by the fact that the novitiate had just been built and required a great deal of cleaning. We spent the majority of our time, outside of a few necessary instructions and daily classes, scouring, washing, picking up debris, sweeping and dusting everywhere; in short, doing all that was necessary to get the place looking like a proper convent. We were the largest group that had ever entered the Community at one time: eighteen of us; and the Sisters remarked that we were specifically sent by God to be a cleaning detail, which they greatly appreciated. By the end of that first year, eight postulants had returned to their homes, and by the end of the second year, there would be only four of us taking vows. I believe this high attrition rate was due partly to the hard physical work, but mostly due to the dawning realization that religious life was far from being a picnic. It was pretty intense, mentally, emotionally and spiritually, every minute of the day. One really had to feel called to this type of life and be able to find contentment in living it.

One activity that we greatly enjoyed was going to choir practice at the end of a hard morning's work. Learning to sing Gregorian Chant was a blessing because it calmed our spirits and filled us (me, anyway) with such joy. At some point, much to our delight, folk songs were introduced in our repertoire; a lovely and welcome change from the more demanding church music.

Life as a novice was not all work and prayer and no play. We were a lively bunch, and would often burst out in laughter over the silliest things: inadvertently dropping a bowl of soup in the middle of the table; pulling out a drawer and causing all the utensils to crash to the floor during a time of silence; making a silly mistake in reading aloud. All these and more were enough to start us giggling, then laughing our hearts out to the point of tears streaming down our faces.

A lot of the over-reaction was due to nervous tension, of course. Part of the difficulty was the intrinsic meaning of why we were in the novitiate in the first place, coming to grips with the questions each of us had to ask: "Am I cut out for this kind of life? Do I really want to spend the rest of my life in the convent? Is this really my vocation?" It was always sad to find out that at any given morning we could find that another one of our group was gone without the novice mistress ever warning us of the imminent departure. There would be another empty seat at table or in choir or wherever, and there was nothing we could do about it, except wonder, "What happened? And who's going to be next?" Because of this, the whole two-year period of training was inevitably fraught with anxiety and suspense. We did have access to talk to the Novice Mistress any time that we needed help, and that was truly a blessing. Still, it always came down to each one's own decision *to stay or not to stay.*

One reason why I seemed to sail through a lot of emotional or mental difficulties was that whenever I came up against some sort of inner problem, I would *always* get the exact word I needed to hear at that moment to bring me back to inner peace. The word could come from a book I was reading, from a person who was speaking, or in any number of ways. I remember sharing this with one of the novices who was troubled and couldn't sleep, and she wistfully replied, "I wish that would happen for me." I felt really sorry that it didn't, and realized how blessed I was.

The assistant to the novice mistress, Sister Amanda, had a very stern, austere exterior, but she was really tender-hearted towards us. While we were strolling one time, she told us about a former novice who had come to her, all troubled about thoughts she was having. Sister had managed to calm her down at the time, and then she said to us, "She *believed* her thoughts, can you imagine?" Then she added: *"Thoughts are not important, period!"* Since these words were spoken by a person in authority I believed them, and was filled with incredible joy and relief in using them as a mantra whenever troublesome thoughts came up.

I continued this practice for a very long time, but gradually, my analytical and judgmental mind took over, and thoughts started troubling me again. I did not realize that I was creating the problem by *believing* my thoughts. And I didn't feel free again until Jesus came to me in chapel a few years later.

DISAPPOINTMENT

I got a real blow to my expectations of becoming a classroom teacher when I was told, no ifs or buts, that because of my many years of taking piano lessons, I would continue my training under the same instructor I'd studied with in school. My fate was sealed: I was to become a piano teacher, the *last* thing in the world I wanted to do. This meant that from the get-go I was separated from the other novices who took classes to eventually become school teachers. I felt isolated as I practiced piano in my little room. I had no real passion for this. It felt very hard to be so alone, and I felt myself being inundated by fears and scruples and anxieties of all sorts. Possibly physical fatigue had something to do with it, too, but I soon broke down and cried and cried. One of the novices who had trained as a nurse was there for me while I went through this hard time. The interesting thing is that I don't think I ever talked about what was troubling me, but somehow the crying was cathartic and within a few days, I was my old self again. I did not remember the specifics of the little crisis, and I soon resumed my duties.

Later, when I began teaching piano, there were aspects of being a music teacher that I especially loved: I had a few older students who practiced diligently and were simply a joy to teach; and then, I absolutely enjoyed directing the Glee Club. Working with groups was exhilarating and right down my alley. I also directed the nuns' choir and became the designated organist. This was the instrument I felt was MY instrument, which was proven to be the case years later when I took organ lessons while at the Motherhouse in Quebec.

Throughout the whole of my novitiate, foremost in my mind and heart was a constant longing for an ever closer relationship with God. As a teenager Father Paul had been instrumental in helping me deepen and shift my focus from fear of sinning, to a more personal, loving, easygoing intimacy with the Father. He had encouraged me to talk to Him as a real person, about anything that came to mind. That way of relating had become very easy and natural for me. I frequently felt peace flooding my heart and was often filled with deep joy.

When I entered the convent, we were told that we needed to develop a relationship with Jesus. After all, we were going to become the brides of Christ. Since I had made up my mind to be the best little novice possible I obeyed every detail that governed my life, *for a while.* So, I switched from relating to the Father, to developing a relationship to Jesus. At the time I did not really know how to connect to Jesus as compared to connecting to the Father and thus lost the easy and comforting closeness to God that had so fed me. This was a huge loss! Still, in some way, that closeness was still there, showing itself in unexpected ways. One time during our morning break I remember running out of the novitiate to greet the beautiful outdoors filled with glee, while crying out loudly and clearly, "Abba Abba Abba!" I had no idea that that word meant "Father." *Years later when I found out, I remembered the look of joy and recognition on my novice mistress's face when she heard* me. She knew the significance of those words, but never shared or ventured to enlighten me or talk with me about it.

I continued obeying everything to the letter of the law, except for this instance: we were expected to work at our perfection. This was to be our main goal throughout our religious life. I soon realized that I *could not do this*. I became very confused and anxious about trying to do the right thing; it was much too much of an incapacitating concern for me. From my own deep knowing I decided to skip that particular command. No one would ever know that I'd changed course because this was all inner work, after all. I decided to emulate St. Therese, whose autobiography I continued to read once a year, and put all my attention and focus *on being as loving as I could be to one and all.*

In my zealous idealism, however, I ended up becoming rigid about what one should do to please God and became a self-righteous and preachy little know-it-all. My letters to my mother and oldest sister became full of religious platitudes. I was more than eager to share my infinite depths of wisdom with them whether they wanted it or not. They never complained, because I was, after all, going to become *the nun*!

After two years of training we became professed Sisters, now part of the greater Community. We'd spent ten days in silent retreat, had our heads shaved the day before the occasion, and taken vows of poverty, chastity and obedience for one year, to be renewed every year for five years, after which we would pronounce final vows binding us to the Community for life.

The day of taking vows was a day of rejoicing with friends and relatives who came to witness the ceremony. This was an exciting time, but also a time of nervous anxiety. No longer were we to live in the gentle bosom of the novitiate, our home for the two previous years. Each one of us was going to a different convent, and we'd been warned that life would not be the same as life in the novitiate. How different could it be, really? After all, we all belonged to the same Community, obeyed the same rules and regulations, prayed and meditated together, had relaxing times together—It couldn't be that dissimilar, could it?

LIFE AS A PROFESSED NUN

The novitiate had been for the most part, relatively easy, and we had vastly enjoyed each other's company. Being a professed nun was quite another matter. It was a real eye opener into the frailties and foibles of human nature. Nuns were generally kind and considerate, so I was surprised and frankly dismayed by the seeming hostility of the nun who greeted me when I first arrived at the convent to which I was assigned. She turned to the Sister Superior who stood next to her and, with a very forbidding look on her face, looked down her nose at me and exclaimed, "*This* is Sister Vivian?" I was literally speechless. What could I say to such a reception? Was this a prelude to what I faced in the coming year? I didn't know, but right then and there I decided to make the best of it by loving her as much as I could. With time, Sister warmed up to me, accepted me, and became downright friendly towards me.

During my first year as a professed nun, I had the opportunity and the freedom to read authors that were more in line with what my soul was looking for. Father Thomas Keating's book on *Centering Prayer,* proved to be a godsend to me: It was exactly what I needed. What he suggested was very simple: to get into deep meditation, all I had to do was breathe in deeply, send the breath to my *stillpoint* (right below the heart) and stay there without thinking, simply centered on that point of stillness. With this method I was plunged into deep peace for a few minutes. I began practicing this after each period of daily group meditation during which a Sister read a few lines from a book on which we were supposed to meditate. This did not work for me, so after the common meditation in chapel was over, I'd wait till every one of the Sisters had left, back up in the corner of the pew, and go inward to that place of profound calmness and remain there as long as I could. Soon I started feeling energy along my whole spine and serenity flooded me. There were no thoughts, just a feeling of soothing emptiness for a while. But when thoughts started coming one after the other I'd stop the meditation, and continue with the day, for I didn't know how else to handle wandering thoughts at the time.

I've since learned how to deal with my thoughts—which I will write about a little further on. Nobody ever knew I was meditating in this way. Without my realizing it I was being guided by Spirit beyond my mind.

That first year I was placed under the supervision of the best piano teacher in the Community. Sister Francine had taught me piano during my high school years, so I thought I knew her. I was really astonished to find her very demanding, authoritarian, and unbelievably stern. This was a side of her I had not seen. I bent over backwards to keep her happy: I'd keep the music room tidy, wash the floor, obey every little order she gave me as perfectly as I could. I did not understand why she seemed to resent me. Then one day she told me, "You will never get a Bachelor's degree in music… *never*!" I realized she saw me as a rival. Sad, for I had no intention of living the rest of my life as a music teacher. I did not reveal this to her for fear of being called to the Provincial Superior's office to explain myself, and perhaps face the option of either obeying blindly or leaving the Community. Sister Francine could have been a much happier person if she had not let jealousy blind her, and I felt sad for her.

At the end of the year I was summoned to the local Superior's office for an end-of-the-year assessment of my time under Sister Francine's supervision. Mother Superior looked at me kindly, and smilingly said, "Sister told me that you don't like to be told what to do." I was really put off. *Of course* I didn't like to have somebody bossing me around all the time, but I obeyed her every wish, didn't I? What else did the woman want? Anyway, I did not argue the point, nor did I try to justify myself. I let the Superior believe what she wanted to believe. She did not reprimand me in any way, and I felt things would eventually work themselves out.

Sure enough, I was sent to a different convent the following year; no more supervision from bossy Sister Francine. What a relief and a blessing! I would be teaching piano and choir on my own and enjoyed the idea of this bit of autonomy to the utmost.

Every time I was commissioned to a new convent, though, I came across some hostility. There was always one nun who, for some reason or other, just didn't like me. Usually being the youngest of the Community made me an easy target for nuns who needed to take out their frustrations and unhappiness on somebody. I soon learned an important lesson: every time this happened, I would step back, and take a look inside to see what I was doing to bring this on. Inevitably I'd realize that what I saw in her was also what I saw in me. I worked on changing my attitude, and sure enough, the Sister would change her behavior towards me. I thought that was pretty wonderful, and I practiced that way of dealing with hostility from then on, always to my great benefit.

Once, however, I felt I needed to stand my ground and speak up to stop the verbal abuse directed at me on a daily basis. I didn't know if this was the *right* thing to do but I decided to do it anyway. This particular Sister was a very grumpy person, and every day when she'd return from her teaching duties, she would accost me wherever I was and shout accusations that had nothing to do with me. I was in a little room giving piano lessons and never even interacted with her during the day! I was simply easy prey, that's all. This one afternoon, though, I stood tall and firm before her, eyed her without blinking, and when she finished, I confronted her in the same tone of voice she'd used with me. I don't remember what I said, but she backed off, physically and emotionally. Stunned by my stance, she quietly turned around and left the room. I never had any trouble with her again. She became friendly and kind and even quite gentle towards me. I felt I'd really done the *right* thing.

I was not always very nice. Far from it; I had my faults and weaknesses and was sometimes inconsiderate. There was one Sister in particular who was extremely kind and helpful to everyone, and I took advantage of her goodness more than once. When we were away from the convent during summer school, we had to send our soiled linen coifs to the Provincial house to get cleaned and starched and sent back to us. Somehow I would always get Sister Veronica to pack mine up with hers, until she finally showed her resentment, and I realized I was really acting like the spoiled brat that some Sisters thought I was. I was expecting Sister to serve me! I recognized that I was behaving very much like my mother then, which, I had promised myself, was something I would *never* do... interesting. I apologized to Sister, and learned to do this bit of necessary packing for myself. Sister forgave me, and we remained very good friends.

One of the ways that I related to God, when I had to deal with very painful menstruation periods, was to turn to Him with the prayer: *"Not my will but Thine be done, dear Father."* Whenever I first moved to a new convent and was assailed with the pain again and again, I would immediately look for the crucifix in the room I happened to be in and repeat the above prayer that Jesus said in his agony, and thus was better able to endure the distress. Another prayer that I used every night for years while kneeling at my bedside, was: *"Father, into your hands I commend my spirit."* I would get into bed, fall into a deep sleep, and wake up refreshed the next morning.

When I finally told my Superior about my awful monthly discomfort, she sent me to a doctor. After three abdominal surgeries that alleviated my discomfort only minimally, I was finally relieved from the distress that had dogged me for years when, at the age of forty two, I had a fourth surgery and the doctors performed a total hysterectomy. What a relief! Then I wondered: Why couldn't the doctors have done this years ago? But of course, it was because they did not want to remove all of my female organs while I was still young enough to bear children, in case I ever left the convent.

THE VISITATION

I had a mystical experience during my fourth year as a nun while living and working at a home for emotionally disturbed children. The home was huge and housed over a hundred children with a large community of nuns caring for them. I so loved those children! When my day of teaching piano was over, I'd volunteer to take care of them. I especially appreciated accompanying them outdoors. They loved to play baseball and enthusiastically encouraged me to play with them. I was never good at sports and had not been able to hit a ball when I was younger, but I spunkily gave it a try. The kids were so thoughtful and caring of me. They would literally make it impossible for me not to hit the ball, run the bases for me, and cheer me on to a homerun. "Y-EA-EA-EAH, Mother Mary Vivian! A HOMERUN!" I had a blast. We had a great relationship, which was a real blessing because it was such a healthy way of releasing tension in my life.

I used to be quite scrupulous, i.e. examine my thoughts obsessively to find out whether or not I'd committed a sin. At this time of my life scruples had become a big problem for me and were depriving me from the peace and happiness that I longed for. I'd also had a fear of negative thoughts from the time that I'd been taught they could become sinful. Probably they kept coming back because I resisted them so much. I kept doing the only thing I knew how to do: control them by blocking them. My confusion kept mounting and my life became pretty dark and fearful. Then, one day I picked up a book by a nun who'd been bedridden for years, entitled *Faith in the Love of God*. After reading the book, absorbing as much of it as I could, I went whole days just repeating the following words over and over again: *"Jesus, I believe in your love for me, but increase my faith."* Even though this prayer did not resound in my heart, I kept at it doggedly for a good two years.

In my third year at the home, I went down to the chapel one day to pray the stations of the cross, to try to find some kind of relief from the scruples and confusion that were threatening to overwhelm me. I felt I was literally on the edge of an abyss and about ready to fall in…

In those days when one joined a Community, one was taught prescribed prayers. You said certain prayers as you woke up, as you put your clothes on, before doing any reading, before meals, etc. So this particular day I had every intention of saying the standard prayers for the stations of the cross as I went from one station to the other.

But this time, I suddenly received the direction to say at each of the fourteen stations these simple words, *"Jesus loves me." As I went from one station to the other, unbelievably, the words became more and more real to me, until, when I got to the last station and knelt at the altar rail, the whole chapel was filled to overflowing with the all-encompassing, palpable, love of God.*

I was surrounded and enveloped and enclosed in this amazing divine love. And then...

All of a sudden, I was kneeling at Jesus's feet with my hands on His lap, looking up into His eyes. There was such a depth of love there that I felt I could go through everything I'd been through, if necessary, for the rest of my life, just to experience that incredible astonishing love again. I wanted to look behind me to see if there was somebody there for whom this awesome love was meant, but no, *there was no one else in chapel.* Then, I wanted to look at my scruples again, thinking, "But, what about... ?" *and Jesus kept pulling me back to look at him,* and I was able to put my negative and dark thoughts aside. *He never said a word, never had to. His eyes drew me like a magnet. I felt that all the human love in the whole world from the beginning of time up to that point was but a spark compared to the huge conflagration of love emanating from Him.* No words can ever describe the feeling of pure joy and ecstasy that filled me to the very depths of my being and exploded in every cell, in every fiber of my body. *When I finally accepted that His love was really and truly meant for me and smiled back at Him, He disappeared.*

I gently got up from the altar rail, and slowly started to walk towards the chapel door, feeling sorry that this incredible experience was over. But it proved to be otherwise, for suddenly...

A Light from beyond the cathedral ceiling of the chapel swiftly and quietly entered my heart and God's infinite, unconditional love took over. That's the only way I can describe it. I was totally filled to overflowing with this great love that coursed through every part of me. There was simply no other reality: thoughts were not real, feelings were not real, there was no more little me! Joy and peace filled me to overflowing, and I couldn't stop smiling. I was in heaven! Still, I remember wondering, Jesus just appeared to me; Who or What is This that's filling me now? God, the Father? The Holy Spirit? Jesus, the Christ? I couldn't figure it out, therefore I forgot about trying to understand, which was the only sensible and wise thing to do. I simply stayed in the experience of God's embrace and all-consuming love in that moment and the next—and the next—and the next—for the next two weeks.

Now I realize that the Father, Son, and Holy Spirit, being One God, may manifest as one or the other; but not being separate from each other, it was the powerful love of this Holy Trinity that filled me to overflowing.

I floated out of chapel, feeling light as air, and proceeded to continue with my everyday duties and chores as though nothing extraordinary had happened. I walked around with a perpetual smile on my face *as incredible love and peace and joy were who and what I was.* I couldn't do enough for the Sisters and the children. I went out of my way to be as helpful as I could even without being asked. I knew that God was loving them through the vessel that I am, and I remember thinking, *"Don't the Sisters see the change in me? Have I always been beaming at everybody like this?"*

I realize now that if they were not aware of anything different in me, it was probably a blessing. I would never have been able to reveal the awesomeness of the experience without diminishing it, and it was probably better that they did not know, since they either would not have believed it, or given me a really hard time about it. In the meantime, I lived in glowing and unbelievable ecstasy for the duration of the experience, which gradually diminished over fourteen days time. I was then twenty-three years old.

Of course, I would have wanted this sublime experience to go on forever. I felt quite bereft when I came back to earth and wondered, *"What am I supposed to do with this incredible occurrence?"* There was no doubt in my mind that the whole experience came from God. One cannot be filled with such love and peace and joy unless it comes from a Source beyond the little self. Again, it was impossible to bring anybody into my confidence. There was no one among the Sisters that I felt I could talk to. We'd been taught in the novitiate of the dangers of mystical experiences! We were told that they could come from the devil; they could come from pride; we were never to give credence to such happenings. I wasn't about to take a chance of being put on the carpet, and being labeled as an emotional misfit (or worse) for the rest of my life.

But, I could continue loving one and all; that was easy enough for me to do for God Himself was doing it. Deep joy and peace still filled me. However, because there was some fear in me of placing too much importance on the mystical aspect of this occurrence I did not make any effort to remember, for instance, what Jesus's eyes looked like, which became a source of regret for me through the years.

Not surprisingly, thoughts again became problematic off and on in the years after this momentous event, because it took me a while to see that believing my thoughts, mistaking them for truth, and paying attention to them, rather than going to my center and reconnecting to God's everlasting, unconditional love would always put me in a state of confusion, worry and doubt.

After a while, I was *dying* to find somebody I could share my experience with. I made a decision to briefly outline what had happened in the privacy of the confessional when I next partook of that sacrament. I figured that because the priest couldn't see me and would not know me, it was relatively safe to talk to him. This was a huge mistake! He blasted me, laughed at me, scolded me, and was totally merciless with me. I came out of that little compartment completely shaken and traumatized. I was so shocked and hurt I just wanted to crawl into some safe place and hide. My heart literally felt as though it had been knifed. Unbelievable searing pain spread through my chest as I stumbled out the chapel door, away from that heartless priest, away from that scathing, painfully injurious denunciation of *the most precious experience of my life*.

Life had to go on. Way down deep, I knew the visitation was real, more real than anything else in the so-called real world. I simply didn't know what to do with it except keep on loving everybody as much as I could, so that's what I did.

One of the great results of the experience was that I had a turn-around in my life where scruples were concerned. They had plagued me for a long time and it was such a relief to be free of them! I also remember that I wanted everybody to know how very much God loved them. I'd see someone in emotional or physical pain and say inwardly, *"If you only knew how much God loves you!"* And I'd love them as best as I could, in whatever way was needed.

I had one huge difficulty around the whole experience at that time. I really didn't get the Big Truth that *what God had done for me was not just for me, but because we are all One, it was done for everyone… ad infinitum.* I did not know this, and not wanting to think of myself as special, I made a habit of staying in the background, being the last one in line, making sure everyone else had the bigger piece of cake, and so on. I wanted the least attention possible.

My life never again got as dark as it did prior to this awesome life-changing occurrence. Still, I was too analytical, too self-absorbed and self-preoccupied, too critical, and too judgmental of myself and others to be as free as I could be and wanted to be in my mind and in my heart. I remember realizing this about myself as a teenager and knowing that I had *to learn to forget myself* if I was ever going to be truly happy. But how does one do this?

I had received some kind of answer to that conundrum shortly after I entered the convent: during my first-ever ten day retreat, the retreat master who was someone from my hometown and whom I greatly respected, shouted at us during one of his sermons, "YOU ARE NOTHING! YOU DON'T COUNT! YOU ARE NOT IMPORTANT!" I felt liberated, I felt free. My thoughts were nothing—They were not important—My feelings were not important—I was not important! I could have jumped up in the middle of the chapel for sheer joy. I wanted to dance and run and sing and shout out to the whole world, "Isn't it great? I'm not important!" And so, whenever a negative thought or feeling came into my consciousness, I repeated this mantra over and over and the thought or feeling disappeared.

I continued this manner of dealing with any unwanted ideas and emotions for over a year, and I felt light and joyous and simply marvelous. Then, at some point, out of the blue, I felt that if I said the mantra one more time, I would fall into an abyss, and perhaps lose part of myself irrevocably—so I backed off. It was difficult for me to reverse direction and refrain from saying the words that had been so healing for me, but at the time I felt it was imperative and necessary to do so. This was one of the times that I wished I had somebody to talk to! But that was not meant to be, and so I kept resolutely on as best as I could.

Near the end of my second year in the novitiate, Sister Amanda told us one day that "thoughts were not important," (see p.52) and that truth had reverberated with me because of my experience of almost two years before on the retreat. Certainly not believing in random or negative thoughts has been one of the major lessons of my life. I'm still working at this but I am happily doing much better with this particular lesson.

THE WONDERFUL YEAR AT THE MOTHERHOUSE

After renewing our vows for the required five years, the time had come for the Sisters of my group to spend a year at the Motherhouse in Quebec before taking final vows, and learn about the different works of the Community. By this time there were only three left of the eighteen who had entered seven years earlier. This was an important and somewhat scary step. Taking vows for life certainly sounded pretty portentous to me. But we went to meet the challenges ahead with bravado and joyfully went off to experience this new adventure in another country. And that's exactly what the whole great year felt like: an exciting undertaking.

Final vows were taken for a lifetime and were not taken lightly. Before the advent of Vatican II there were very few nuns who had asked to be released from their vows. I remember only one nun in my Community who took that step in the years before such a move was tolerated. She was very popular, very beautiful inside and out, and very well loved. All of a sudden, one day, we realized she was not around anymore. Because she'd made the decision to leave, she was considered a pariah, a person putting herself in danger of eternal damnation. Since the Superiors did not want this "disease" to spread throughout the Community, we were not allowed to say our goodbyes to her or wish her godspeed. I felt that such treatment of a woman who'd given a good part of her life (she was in her 40s) to the service of the Community, was incredibly insensitive and unfair, but that's the way it was, and there was nothing one could do about it except hope that some day common sense and Christian charity would prevail in the Community.

During our year at the Motherhouse we visited all the institutions where the Sisters worked, and then each one of us went to help out in one of them. I so much enjoyed working with the tough little teenage girls under my care; there was something really special about them. Life had dealt them some hard blows, but they were on the rebound, and they mostly wanted to be loved and given a chance to start a new life, which was made possible by the Sisters who cared for them. Unfortunately, one of the girls got a crush on me from the first time we met. Marie did not understand that the relationship could not be a lasting one and ended up being very angry with me. (In my Community, Sisters were not allowed to have friendships with lay people, no matter the circumstance.) I had to use tough love with her, which I've always found extremely difficult to do. Nevertheless, it sometimes becomes the *only* path to take, and usually turns out to be the best way of dealing with certain situations.

Life with the young Canadian Sisters at the Motherhouse was anything but dull. In fact we enjoyed each other so much and had so much fun that I knew it would be hard to leave at the end of the year. The Canadians were so much more relaxed about rules and regulations than we Americans were. We'd say, half jokingly, that the Canadian Sisters wrote the rules, and we Americans obeyed them. No doubt about it.

We never knew what kind of retreat master we'd end up having to listen to once a year, but usually they were good, and sometimes very good. I sensed that like us, many priests were searching for the Truth which came from another place than the Vatican. This was 1956; it would be another six or seven years before the advent of Vatican II when good Pope John XXIII would "open the windows wide" to create changes in the Church and purge it of old paradigms that were totally inflexible and detrimental to the people under the Church's tutelage. The need for deep changes was starting to be felt among many of the clergy, religious, and lay people. Hope was in the air and we young nuns felt the excitement of it. It was a great time to be alive; so much was possible! How far would our own Community be willing to go to make meaningful and practical changes? Only time would tell.

The very best thing that happened to me during my year at the Motherhouse was receiving organ lessons on the Casavant Organ, one of the very finest organs in Canada, which happened to be in the chapel of the Motherhouse. Sister Gabrielle, the organist, was a warm-hearted, dear person. She was also an excellent teacher and a fabulous musician, and I couldn't have asked for a better mentor. I got a weekly lesson from her and learned to be as proficient in using my feet as I was with my hands to produce the most glorious music possible. The sounds coming from that organ were astonishing and I basked in the wonderful vibrations that coursed through my body as I played. This was such tremendous fun! Sister was very encouraging, saying that soon I'd be playing as well as she did; and that is exactly what happened. After a while the Sisters seated in the chapel below couldn't differentiate my playing from hers. Best of all she was not jealous, but continued to praise and inspire me throughout that whole wonderful year. I loved her and I loved to play the organ and I loved my Canadian Sisters. I would have stayed in Canada forever if I'd been allowed to do so, but this was not an option. I was still needed as a piano teacher in the Massachusetts convent, and therefore would have to return to the states when the time came.

An added benefit to our year spent at the Motherhouse was the really great opportunity to brush up on our French. The young Canadian nuns got quite a kick out of the way we spoke, often exclaiming, "Oh, is *this* what you mean?" Then insert the correct word, and we'd laugh hilariously at the joke of it all. Under the tutelage of our young friends it was amazing how quickly our French improved. When I next came in contact with members of my family, though, I learned that speaking Quebec French sounded very snobbish to them, therefore I resorted to speaking patois so as not to appear "better than."

Strange to say, the Sisters who taught in my hometown were mostly English speaking and didn't appreciate our French heritage. They never gave us cause to be proud of our Canadian forebears, and were often hard and unkind to children who spoke with a heavy French accent. It was not surprising that people like my father felt so inferior about the way they spoke. How could it be otherwise?

It was not until many years after I'd left the area, that a Van Buren native who'd studied Quebec French extensively, returned and taught the young people about their own rich culture. Finally, speaking with a French accent became acceptable, and something about which one didn't have to be ashamed. At this point in time I know that the older people in town still speak French, but the young people do not; it is difficult for them to see any value of it in our American way of life.

FALLING IN LOVE

Two years after pronouncing perpetual vows I had a totally uncalled for and unexpected experience: I fell in love. Oh my God! Why did this have to happen when I'd just made my final promises? This couldn't happen to me. What was I going to do about it? This was totally insane. How did it happen? And for the first time in my life I found out what an infatuation was like.

Before school began that memorable year, I went to my classroom to get the room ready for my first day of teaching. I was going down the steps when I saw this young man coming up the steps from the floor below. He was a new teacher in school whom I hadn't met. I smiled at him and greeted him cordially, and he smiled back without saying a word. I turned around to look at him while I continued going downstairs and saw that he'd also turned around to look at me. *Hmm-mm,* I thought, *interesting.* At recess time that day, I spotted him way across the yard as he spotted me. Every day from then on, while we stayed with our respective classes, no matter where we were, our eyes would meet, and we'd beam at each other. We were drawn together like magnets, and this went on and on and on. I told the Lord that *this was terrible and most inconvenient.* Why couldn't this have happened *before* I took the plunge of pronouncing vows for life? It was no laughing matter: I couldn't sleep, my appetite was gone, and I became very clumsy when I saw him. One of my assignments was teaching music in the classrooms that year, and whenever I entered his classroom, I lost it. I'd drop the eraser, sheets of paper, anything I held in my hand, and awkwardly bend down to retrieve the item, feeling myself blush furiously. I noticed that the students were grinning. They suspected what was going on, the clever ones, though they never said a word. And what was John doing? Looking at me with roguish eyes and a mischievous grin on his face—the blooming idiot! We never said more than a "Good morning"—"Good afternoon" to each other and I really didn't understand what was stopping him from approaching me at recess time simply to have a conversation. Since all the other nuns were outside at that time, I couldn't very well take the first step towards him without their noticing and drawing their own conclusions, could I?

This went on for most of the school year and I was miserable and had had more than enough of this nonsense. So, one day I decided to take the initiative and find out what was going on with the man. I took a risk and placed a note in his mail slot at school asking him to meet me at lunch time on a certain day when a certain classroom stood empty. Thus it was that towards the end of winter, when it was still pretty cold, I trundled up the stairs to the vacant classroom all bundled up in shawl and hood for a rendezvous with destiny—or what?

I waited and waited and waited, and finally there was a knock on the door. To my "Come in!" John slowly strolled in, silently closing the door behind him. He was still wearing an incredible smile on his handsome face, but again said nothing—*nada*—*rien du tout*. I started talking, asking questions, waiting for a response. Nothing. I tried desperately to open the conversation, but he remained close-mouthed. Finally, in exasperation, I walked to the door, placed my hand on the doorknob, only to hear the man speak his first words, "I spoke to my spiritual director about you." I was beside myself with indignation. He could speak to his spiritual director but he couldn't say a word to *me?* What a wimp! Enough already. There would be no more eye contact or smiles from across the yard. I'd had it. I don't think I even turned back to look at him as I went through the door and closed it. I was upset, angry, and felt terribly young, foolish and embarrassed. As far as I was concerned this was the finale. The end. Period.

But no, the stupid man kept sending me signals, and though I was sure that I was through with him, I couldn't help but smile back at him. Ridiculous! Ultimately, I did the only reasonable thing: I went to my Mother Superior, told her what had been going on, and requested that she ask the Mother Provincial to send me to a new post in the fall. This Mother Superior was a very broadminded and commonsensical person. She listened to me, did not question my honesty or integrity, and took the matter in hand. Thankfully, in the fall, I was duly commissioned to another convent and school. Problem solved quickly and easily.

During the following school year, I learned that John was a seminarian studying for the priesthood who'd taken a sabbatical leave because he was unsure of his vocation, and he'd landed in the school where I was teaching to test the waters. That explained his behavior a bit, but in my eyes he was still a wimp.

A few years later, I happened to be visiting at the same convent I'd been in when I met John. I was told that he'd recently been ordained to the priesthood and that he was coming to greet the Sisters that very afternoon in the schoolhouse where we'd met. By that time, the Community had changed from the old religious habit to a freer, lighter dress, which went down to mid-calf rather than to the floor. I lined up with the other Sisters to greet him and congratulate him. I was curious to see how he looked and if he would recognize me. He was sitting behind a table in the room, greeting each Sister in turn, and saying a few words to each one. Oh my, I thought, surprise! He can talk. As I stood in front of him, *he looked me up and down slowly and deliberately.* I couldn't believe his nerve! Mentally, I fumed: "You feel very safe now that you're hiding behind a roman collar, don't you. How dare you look at me that way!" I felt insulted and demeaned, but was also thoroughly convinced that I'd made the right decision a few years back and was so glad and proud of myself that I had not let my infatuation get the best of me.

I believe this was a necessary experience for me because it gave me an idea of how easy it is to mistake the "falling in love" stage for the real thing. Even with my strong commitment to Christ I could still be vulnerable to good looks and a warm smile. I was and still am, after all, very human. Though the whole episode had been uncomfortable and painful, it was a really important lesson for me and served me very well in later years when I started looking for a soul-mate.

A BREATH OF FRESH AIR AND FATHER TOM

With the advent of Vatican II under the reign of dear old Pope John XXIII who opened the windows wide to air out the insides of the Church, some of us nuns greatly rejoiced and looked forward to the new decrees sent out to religious congregations. We were now actually allowed to ask for different kinds of work if we so desired. I definitely so desired. Although I'd had a number of excellent pupils through the thirteen years I'd been teaching piano, I'd had plenty of kids whose mothers were the ones who wanted their children to play, and so the kids, naturally, never practiced. I looked forward with glee to trying my skills at something else and finally got the opportunity to switch to teaching in a classroom.

My first teaching assignment was not in a regular classroom at all. I was sent to replace an older nun in a school that taught religion to kids after school hours and on Saturdays. One of the nuns also visited needy parishioners in their homes. This particular Community of nuns had been made up of the same four nuns for five years, and I was coming in to replace one of them. It ended up being the most difficult year I ever experienced as far as the convent living situation was concerned. (*Watch out what you ask for.*)

I knew I was in for a challenging time when, on opening the door to receive me, only one of the three nuns gave me the traditional kiss of peace: a kiss on both cheeks. Oh oh, I thought, this is going to be an interesting year. The Superior, who was older in years than I was, but younger in religious life, determined that I was in need of discipline and correction. Every single evening after supper, she would use some pretext to make me cry. I soon caught on that the sooner I cried, the sooner the whole ordeal would be over; she'd be satisfied that she'd taught me a lesson and I was then fit to join the other Sisters for recreation. One of the other two nuns was jealous of any kind of creative work I did, whether for my classroom or in the convent dwelling, so I dispensed with making creative decorations and such, to try to keep her happy. The third nun was a spy: I don't know how she did it, but she knew of my every move. I dared not write to my Provincial Superior to let her know what was going on, because this nun would somehow find out about it and I'd have hell to pay.

I did what I had been trying to do all of my convent life: I smiled and loved them in every way I could, all the while telling the Lord at every hard step of the way, *"Lord, I believe in your love for me."* It was strange, but the more loving I was towards them, the more they became resentful of me. Things never got better, and I bore the emotional abuse as bravely as I could for the remainder of the school year. This situation was not going to last forever, after all.

During the ten-day retreat that fall, I was able to meet with the Provincial Superior and tell her what had been going on. I asked her to please transfer me to another convent the coming year. "Send me anywhere you want, but back there," I asked. She believed me unwaveringly, and she did not send me back.

The priest who was the preacher at that retreat was a Franciscan and was absolutely beautiful. I loved his sermons; they were so full of wisdom. I resolved to go talk with him. I had developed the habit of speaking with the current spiritual retreat master every year (if he was any good) because I felt that was one way of letting off steam. It was good for my soul and for my emotional well-being. It was 9 p.m. on the last day of the retreat when I got in to see Father Tom. I entered the room and he noticed right away that I was tired, so he suggested that I write to him instead of staying up to speak with him. He gave me his address and then said, "Before you leave, why don't I give you my blessing." *Unexpectedly, I received another visitation*: As I knelt down in front of him he started with the formal blessing, "*May the blessing of Almighty God, the Father, Son, and Holy Spirit...*" and I blacked out. *I found myself in a place of complete darkness, standing on the edge of a cliff, looking down, seeing nothing except blackness all around; I was in total peace, and felt absolutely no fear. I wondered, "Is this what God is... Nothing?"* Then suddenly I was back in the room, still kneeling and with eyes closed, wearing this big smile on my face. *I opened my eyes and light was streaming out of them. Father had backed off to the far wall and was surrounded by light.* I felt totally embarrassed and discomfited and closed my eyes again. When I got up I avoided looking at him and quietly, slowly, turned around and walked out the door towards the chapel. I heard Father opening the door, calling to me, "Sister, Sister!" But I paid him no mind, and kept on walking. I went into chapel and very soon I was filled with doubts. What really happened here? Am I imagining things? Was that light really coming from my eyes? Was I again the recipient of God's favoritism? I was still so afraid of thinking myself as "special." I left the chapel and went to bed with my confusion and anxiety rather than retrace my steps and go talk to Father Tom about what had transpired.

Father Tom would have been the perfect priest to open up to, but at the time I was still not ready for that. Years later, I came across him in a gathering for contemplatives and sat down in front of him to ask if he remembered me. He answered, "Of course." Then he said, *"You don't think that experience came from me, do you?"* I replied, *"No."* And that's all I needed to know: I hadn't made it up.

THE CHARISMATIC MOVEMENT

Finally in the fall of 1966 I found myself in a regular classroom. I started off teaching elementary grades, then two years later, in 1968, taught junior high: seventh and eighth grades.

One day in early autumn, Helen, one of the girls in my classroom came to me at the end of class and told me about a very significant experience that her older brother at Notre Dame College had had the previous year. He told his whole family about it, got them enthused over it, and they started going with him to the weekly prayer meetings that were taking place at a nearby Franciscan college. Helen invited me to go with her and her family to one of these prayer meetings. I smiled and said, "I don't think so—but thank you." Helen persisted. Every week she'd approach me with the same request and I always said, "No, thanks." Finally, I got up the courage to ask Mother Superior if I could go and attend one of the sessions and find out what it was all about. She gave me her permission without any hassle. Good sign, I thought.

Thus I embarked on a new aspect of prayer life that was new, different, quite powerful, and turned out to be a great adventure.

Off I went that evening, in the company of this beautiful family, so excited to have me join them. I was looking forward to the evening's session and meeting the priest in charge, Father Ray, and getting to know a whole new group of people and experience how they related to God and to each other.

When we entered the room set aside for the meeting at the College, I was warmly welcomed as I sat down among this very lively group. Father Ray started the evening with spontaneous prayer which elicited enthusiastic responses such as "Praise God," "Thank you, Jesus," and "Alleluia." This was very new to me. We Catholics did not usually pray out loud like this. Father then spoke about the fresh wave of enthusiasm among some members of the clergy for this new movement going on within the Catholic Church. Then the meeting continued with a period of silent meditation. Next, individuals were invited to sit in a chair to be prayed over by having hands placed on their shoulders as the petitioner asked the Lord for healing and for the coming of the Spirit. The rest of us joined in by asking the Spirit to fill us, melt us, mold us and use us in whatever way was needed.

After the prayer session was over, the group burst into joyous song, filling the room with marvelous harmonies, bodies gently swaying with the lively rhythms, hands and arms dancing in the air. It was incredibly soul-stirring and uplifting. We left the premises looking forward to returning in a week's time and experiencing many more such wondrous meetings in the foreseeable future. I was thrilled to have found people who were not afraid of expressing their love for God and who were so full of joy. This was very different from the attitude that prevailed in the convent where we were never encouraged to talk spirituality during recreation since it was thought we prayed enough during the day.

This new movement in the Catholic Church called the Charismatic Movement, had been started in the late 1960s by priests teaching at Notre Dame University in Indiana. Here's how it came about:

A group of priests on campus who felt something was missing in their priestly lives had come together to discuss how the mission given by Jesus to his disciples to teach and heal could be implemented in a more realistic and fulfilling manner in today's world. They asked, *"Isn't Jesus still with us? Aren't we His disciples? What's lacking in our understanding of the ministry? Why can't we use the same gifts that Jesus bequeathed to His followers after His Resurrection?"* In their search for valid and meaningful answers they met with some Pentecostal ministers in the area who, the priests understood, had been successfully using the gifts of the Holy Spirit in their ministry *in the way intended by Jesus,* for many years.

The Pentecostals met with the priests several times, sharing with them the formula they used to bestow the gifts of the Spirit on those people who were open to receiving, and which could prove so effective and beneficial for themselves and for others.

The priests practiced what they'd learned and experienced the benefits of this new movement in their own lives. They enthusiastically shared their excitement with other priests and then proceeded to begin a group of Catholic Pentecostals, right there on campus, inviting students to come and see for themselves the wonders that the Spirit was working among His people. Many of the students became interested in finding out what their teachers were so enthused about, and soon the seven gifts: prophecy, tongues, interpretation of tongues, healing, discernment, wisdom and knowledge, became available to them and to the people close to them.

There were four gifts that were most commonly employed: the gift of discernment: a way of finding out if something came from God or not; the gift of tongues: practiced mainly for the edification of the one using it; the gift of prophecy: the special ability to receive and communicate a message from God; and the gift of healing; on the physical, spiritual, and emotional levels. Most of the time, people would simply feel more at peace with themselves and their world after being prayed over.

The charismatic priests, now filled to overflowing with the joy and promise that these gifts gave them of really making everything new, lost no time in spreading the good news far and wide. Hundreds, maybe thousands of people were already part of the movement when I became involved with it in 1968. Amazingly, much to my delight, I had no trouble getting permission to attend the meetings every week. I felt incredibly blessed and truly and willingly hooked.

Around the feast of Pentecost, some time in May of 1969, the prayer group was invited to attend a lecture by a Dutch Reformed minister, taking place at the Franciscan Monastery. My family of friends invited me along, but I was not allowed to go to this particular meeting by myself because it was happening late at night. Listening to a minister who was outside of the Catholic Church was also a concern. Among all the Sisters, there was one that I felt I could approach and ask to accompany me. Sister Angela was motherly, warm, intelligent, and most importantly, had a terrific sense of humor. She agreed. And so on a warm spring evening we joined our friends in their car, which was full to capacity now, and headed off for an adventure.

We arrived late. The lecture had begun, so we quietly sat down and listened. The talk was not what I had expected at all. The minister was talking about receiving the Baptism of the Spirit and the gift of tongues. I thought of Sister sitting next to me and inwardly cringed. She had no idea what he was talking about. She'd never heard of anything like this in her life, and I was afraid I might really be in trouble when we returned to the convent.

When we took our seats, there was a woman sitting directly opposite me who gave me a friendly smile. Every once in a while I'd look up and catch her looking at me. I was not uncomfortable with her attention and did not attach any importance to it.

It was close to 10 p.m. when the minister said we would take a break. He then suggested that anyone interested in learning more about receiving the gift of tongues could go into the little side room to the right, and he'd meet them there. The rest of the group would spend that time in prayer. I turned to Sister Angela and said, "Let's stay here, shall we?" She was fine with that. But as I watched the people get up and leave for the other room, I changed my mind, "It would be interesting to find out about it, don't you think?" Again, she agreed. So we got up to go. I noticed that the woman who'd been eyeing me, also stood up and followed Sister and me.

Upon entering the room, we found the minister huddled with a dozen or so people around him. I sat down, and the woman who'd followed us in, sat down next to me. Sister Angela went to sit at a place on the side. The minister was talking about preparing oneself physically to receive the gift, "Open your mouth as wide as you can and give a long 'aaaah' sound," he explained. We all did as he asked—I, for one, feeling pretty foolish. "Do this a couple more times, then say the name of Jesus over and over again, and gradually and easily let your tongue make any sound that wants to come out," he finished. I obediently did as he'd told us. The woman next to me asked, "Do you have the gift of tongues?" I replied in the negative. "Would you like to receive it?" I hesitated, then took the plunge: why not? I gave her a 'yes' nod and she stood up behind me, placed her hands on my shoulders and prayed over me. *All at once my throat just opened up! What came out of my mouth sounded like gibberish to me, but at the same time, I was filled with this indescribable abundance of overflowing joy and peace. I had a smile on my face that seemed there to stay, and the woman expressed her excitement by exclaiming, "She's got it!" and called the minister to come and listen for himself.*

The minister bent over to hear what I was saying, and said, "I want you to go sit next to your Sister so she can hear you." I got up and went to Sister Angela's side, but I could not let the "strange tongue" come out for her. I made the decision, wisely, I think, not to obey him. Before we left, the minister came to me with a message, "From now on, I want you to pray in tongues every morning every day of your life." I smiled, but never said I would, and my rebellious side thought, Huh! you're not about to tell *me* what to do for the rest of my life.

Actually, I enjoyed using this gift for it was very helpful in my prayer life. I would begin every meditation by praying in tongues, quietly of course, and I would quickly and easily become centered. From that time on, the prayer of praise and thanksgiving was continually in my heart, and often on my lips, in words or in song. Praying for others consisted of calling the Lord's attention to a person, not even mentioning what the person wanted, then praising and thanking Him for the answer received. It was simple and effective, and I remembered that it was the way that St. Therese of the Child Jesus had taught her novices to pray, and which I'd emulated from the first time I'd ever pondered her words. It was easy and comforting to resume this method of prayer.

In the car on our way back to the convent, every person except Sister Angela had at one time or another received the gift of tongues. Not one of these delightful, lively young women used the gift on the way home out of respect for Sister. I was very impressed by their consideration and thoughtfulness.

Sister Angela was also most thoughtful and considerate of me. She could have gone to Mother Superior the next day and said, "Guess what Vivian has got herself into?" She didn't. She never brought it up with me, either. God bless you, Sister Angela, now in heaven. You are a sweetheart.

It was quite late when Sister and I tiptoed into the convent and to our respective rooms. In those days, we slept three to a room, with only curtains between us for privacy. I got into bed, and as soon as I lay down, the tongues got going. I felt immense joy and couldn't stop smiling and muttering. After a long time I told the Lord, "Hey, stop it! I've got to teach tomorrow." And I went to sleep. The next morning, after my students were all seated, I opened my mouth to speak, and what came out but *gibberish*. I stopped as soon as I realized what was happening, smiled at my pupils who were looking at me open-mouthed, and simply continued with what I had meant to say.

Thank God, the "gift of tongues" behaved and never again came out of my mouth unless I wanted to use it.

Some of my junior high students could be quite rambunctious and rowdy at times. There was one boy in particular who was high strung, couldn't stop moving and was always standing up in the middle of a lesson to say whatever he had on his mind. One evening, while preparing my classes, he came to mind, and after asking for help from the Lord in dealing with him, some silly words came to me, which I employed very effectively the following day. When Roger again stood up I said: *"Hey, honeybunch sweetheart piccalilli sugarplum sweetiepie carrot soup alleluia, would you please sit down?"* This worked like a charm. The look of surprise on his face, as well as on the other children's faces, as he stood with mouth wide open, and rendered speechless, was priceless! He quietly sat down and behaved for the rest of the period. I used these words over and over again with him and other difficult students as needed, and it always worked. Laughter was so healing and so much easier than getting angry, impatient or frustrated; it released tension, prevented me from making mountains out of molehills, and created a long-lasting bond between my dear pupils and me.

DAD'S PEACEFUL DEPARTURE

In 1969, I went to sit by my dear Father's bedside along with my mother, a few of my siblings and a sister-in-law, to spend some time with him during his final days. I prayed for his healing, but he assured me that he was reconciled to leaving his earthly home. He was ready to go. When he'd finally gone to be checked by the doctor, cancer had metastasized throughout his body to the extent that the doctor could not tell where it had begun. He'd borne incredible pain without complaining; he was so tough! He wanted nothing to do with the cobalt treatment that was used in those days and wanted to die at home. So my sister, Joan, who was a nurse, left her home in Maryland with her three children, to come and care for my father. She and my younger brother's wife, Rena, took care of him day and night for three long months. Bless their loving hearts.

Dad went home to God a few days after Thanksgiving in 1969. He was seventy-two years old. I had been staying at my older brother, Jimmy's house, not even a quarter of a mile away, and had gone to have lunch with his wife, Irma, when the phone call came that he was going fast: I hurried over to the house to find that Dad was still with us, but barely breathing. Within a minute or two, he was gone.

Dad may have left his body behind, but as far as I was concerned, he was still around. Once when I dreamed of him he smilingly stated, *"You want to dance, don't you?"* He knew how I adored dancing. When I said *"Yes!"* my older brother, Jimmy, appeared from nowhere, pulled aside an entire wall so we had plenty of space, and Dad and I danced and danced to a beautiful waltz. He was an excellent dancer; we twirled and swooped and he bent me way down and lifted me up and we went round and round and round. It was so much fun! How happy and comforted I felt. Heaven will be just great, I thought.

After Dad was gone, my mother did not feel she could live alone, so my dear brother, Don, and his beloved wife, Rena, left their apartment home to go live with Mom in the family home. Don and Rena had no children, so at the time, that seemed the best possible action to take. It was a very heroic and difficult task to commit themselves to, for my mother was not an easy person to live with. She had not given up her autocratic, self-centered ways, and my brother often found himself having to choose between his wife and his mother, not an easy task, and eventually he became ill.

That arrangement lasted for twelve long years, until Mom left for the Nursing Home in the area, where, it seemed, she was enjoyed by nurses and patients alike during the six years that she lived there before her own departure for the heavenly realms.

THE EFFECTS OF THE GIFTS OF THE SPIRIT

Back in my convent in Lawrence, MA, I continued going to prayer meetings on a weekly basis. But something started happening: the older members of the group who oversaw the meetings told me they thought I had received the gift of healing. I would not acknowledge this. I didn't want the responsibility that would come with this gift, plus, I didn't exactly say so, but I was always afraid of my ego taking over. That was a danger that I thought could so easily happen. The leaders, though, kept after me to accept what was occurring. For weeks I refused them, until finally, one evening, I simply gave in, and thus became part of the healing group that prayed over people during the weekly meeting.

The elders of the assembly confided that people were receiving healing through me. They didn't go into details, and I didn't ask for any. I do remember one man who smilingly told me that his ear problem was gone. Mostly, people felt very peaceful after a session, gave me a great big smile and thanked me. I would gratefully acknowledge them, but never asked for details. After all, I was simply an instrument being used by the Spirit; the Spirit was the healer, not me.

Some years later, after I'd become a massage therapist and developed a clientele, I realized that giving massages was like the "laying on of hands" that I'd practiced when I prayed over people as a member of the Charismatic movement. I also started using more energy work in my practice, such as Harmonic Overtoning, some Reiki, Touch for Health, Quantum touch, and breathing into the painful areas of the body. How wonderful to know that this work could be a way of using the healing gift that I'd received without attaching religion to it. And so it happened that people often felt huge relief from back, shoulder, neck, leg, or foot pain, after a massage, or experienced deep peace and contentment. I had one person who came for just one massage. I bumped into her years later and she told me that the massage had changed her life. It was lovely to hear, for I didn't know if a person was being helped unless the individual chose to tell me. Gradually, through word of mouth, my practice grew significantly larger, and many people became steady clients. That was evidence enough of the worthiness and merit of my work.

I remember one gentleman who came to me for a massage every year after he came back from Florida. One time, I opened the door to receive him and saw that he was almost bent in two from pain because of years and years of golfing. His doctors had told him that the only thing left to do was surgery. I had him lie face down on the table, touched his lower back and could not believe how many adhered fibers I felt on both sides of his spine. I worked the tangled muscles with my fingers for quite a while, then applied a compress of hot cider vinegar and cayenne pepper on the afflicted area and let it do its work. After the session was over he got up from the table and was pleasantly surprised to be able to walk with very little pain. Two days later he came back for one more treatment, after which he felt well enough to resume golfing for the rest of the summer.

The other day, two of my dear friends, Bill and Emery, who had been faithful clients of mine for years until they moved too far away to come to me, picked me up for lunch. We spent an enjoyable two hours reminiscing and sharing. At one point, Bill reminded me of the time when he'd come to me with a very sore arm. He'd been to the chiropractor several times without getting any relief. He could hardly move his arm. "And," he said, "after you'd worked on me for ten minutes, the pain was all gone." He lifted his arm and exclaimed, "I was free!" I had not remembered that, but it was good to hear so many years after the fact.

After my own experience of the Baptism of the Spirit, I felt Jesus's hand on my shoulder off and on for a whole year. I knew the touch came from Him because peace and joy would immediately fill me. And for years I would periodically see Him at the foot of my bed when I was struggling with my thoughts or feelings. He would gently and lovingly smile at me, and whatever had been troubling me would evaporate. For days and weeks afterward, whenever my thoughts tried to get a hold of me, I'd recall His look, and that was all I needed to get back to my center. Often, while at prayer in chapel, I would see Him standing before me, then turn sideways to look behind Him. I gathered He was signaling me to pay attention to the Father, the One behind all of creation, from whom every blessing comes. Once, years later, when I was having a particularly hard time, I saw Jesus on my left side, wearing that same look of Love, but this time beaming at me with a mischievous smile. I couldn't help but feel tickled as I looked up at him and remarked, "*You*

think this is funny, don't you?" He did. And after a while, I did too. I recognized that I was making much ado about nothing, let it go, and grinned along with Him.

In the following years my spiritual experiences sometimes felt like Eastern mysticism to me. Once, while on retreat by myself, I was eating a breakfast of Kellogg's 19 Cereal when I looked out the window and saw the bushes outside glowing with a bright and intense yellow light. I looked down to continue eating, but there was no glowing light inside the room. I looked out again, and the light was still there! As I kept on eating a very clear message came through: *"Everything is sacred."* Every bite I chewed was sacred, every swallow, every action I used to eat, was sacred. I was in this place of deep stillness, savoring every morsel, every moment of this experience, and without any effort on my part, forty-five minutes went by without my even noticing. Upon finishing breakfast, the thought came: "What am I supposed to do with this? There's no way that I can spend forty-five minutes eating breakfast every day. What does this mean, anyway?" This was so far removed from anything I'd been taught in the Catholic Church that I didn't have a clue, so I just left it alone. I never forgot it though, and later on when I learned more about the teachings of both the eastern and western mystics, I was able to connect this experience to the teaching that we are not separate, but one in God and with all things. *Everything is sacred because everything is in God, as God is in everything.*

This incident brought to mind the teachings from Jackie, years earlier, who had taught us to say, "Hi God!" to everyone and everything as we greeted the new morning on awakening, implying that indeed *everything is sacred because everything is a manifestation of God.*

FINDING A JOB ON MY OWN

After two years of being actively involved in the Charismatic movement I became quite disenchanted with what was going on among the leaders of the group. They were engaged in a power struggle that was getting quite nasty and totally contrary to what the movement was all about. I got pretty disillusioned with the whole thing and with the Provincial Superior's encouragement, I eventually left the area and started looking for work on my own, since the Community did not have a job for me at that time.

I looked around for a couple of months while residing in the Provincial house in Saco, Maine. One day I was reading the monthly diocesan paper and came across an article that caught my eye. There was a priest in the northern part of Maine who had opened up a Christian Life Center (affectionately called the "Holy Hut") for high school students of every school in Aroostook County, which was home ground to me. Father Stephen was creating weekend encounters and was looking for a helper to co-ordinate the events and assist in preparing the materials needed to inspire the teenagers. I thought I might as well give it a try. I called him, told him I was interested in the position, and we talked back and forth about what would be required of me and what I could expect from him. He seemed satisfied with my answers and invited me to come and see if we could work together. I gladly jumped at the chance. It seemed the very thing I'd enjoy doing.

I worked with Father Stephen for two years. It was my first time working with high school kids and I enjoyed them and the work tremendously. I had the freedom to be creative in preparing the programs for each weekend, and Father was open to trying out new things. We had a team of lay people who helped put together activities geared to helping the boys and girls express their questions and doubts about their Catholic upbringing without fear of reprimand. For many of the kids this was the first time they were exposed to adult Christians and a priest and nun with whom they felt at ease. They realized that we were human! And they loved us as much as we loved them. The program was varied and well-balanced between serious learning and more relaxed activities. There were fun exercises to do, wonderful uplifting music to sing and dance to, as well as opportunities to get some good positive lessons about living their lives as productively as possible. Long lasting friendships were created between staff, between the teenagers themselves, and between staff and the youngsters.

At the end of the first year at the Center, the staff decided to have a party. It took place at the home of a couple who "parented" the teenagers on weekends. Somebody picked me up and I looked forward to an evening of fun with these young people that I'd grown to know and love so much throughout the year. After a while, drinks were passed out and they offered me one that was mainly seven-up with a little vodka. Not being used to drinking (this was my first time ever), I drank it too fast and started feeling a little fuzzy. Upon mentioning this to the audience at large, one of the boys got me another drink of seven-up, which I again drank too fast. "Hmm-m," I said, "my head is feeling even fuzzier." "Don't worry, Sister, another time should do the trick." And so I imbibed once again. What happened next was that I couldn't put two words together without giggling; everything was so funny! I knew then that I was probably tipsy, and I have to admit that I enjoyed the feeling. I was really having fun! I didn't let on I realized they'd been spiking my seven-up every time they brought me a glass. They thought they were putting one over on me, and I let them enjoy their little game. When it was time to leave, I asked somebody to help me stand up and walk me to the car, laughing all the way as I said my goodnights to one and all. I went to bed that night and slept like a log until daybreak. The following morning, the parent-mother called to ask how I felt: "Did you sleep well?" "I sure did," I replied. "You weren't sick?" "No, why?" "Well," she said, "they put different kinds of liquor in your drink each time they filled your glass. I was afraid you'd be *really sick!*" Stalwart little me had never even felt a twinge of nausea. But the joke was on me, after all. I'd had no idea they'd been putting any other liquor than vodka in my seven-up.

My time at the Holy Hut gave me the opportunity to meet with some nuns from a different Community living in the same town as the Center. Their vocation director, Sister Mary, came once a year to talk to the girls in school about the experience of life in her Community. I found this nun very delightful and very authentic. She even smoked cigarettes! Not that I had any inclination to do that, but I found it most interesting that she was that free. I had some very good talks with her, which later proved to be very useful and helpful for me.

It is now over forty years since the Holy Hut experiment began, and the work is still going on today, though at a new location and with a different director. Thankfully, Father Stephen's work has endured and is still thriving in spite of all the ups and downs and inevitable lacunas and imperfections associated with being part of our human condition.

EXPERIENCING DIFFERENT TYPES OF COMMUNITIES

Through all my years in the convent, every once in a while I'd get a strong feeling that I did not belong there, but that I had to wait for the right time to leave. I felt that when that time came, I would know it without a doubt. (I had no idea it would be a thirty-year wait!) In the meantime, I searched. One of the things I will be ever grateful for is that my Superiors allowed me to investigate other types of Communities that I felt attracted to.

One summer I spent seven weeks at a Community called Madonna House in Combermere, Ontario, Canada. Priests and lay people, both men and women, lived and worked there as part of the Community or as visitors. I'd read the life story of the woman who started the Community, Baroness Catherine von de Hueck Doherty and had been greatly impressed by her life and the work she was doing. She'd founded Friendship Houses in Canada and in the U.S.A. and had been invited by the bishop of Ontario to start a community that would see to the needs of the poor in a very rural area. As her followers grew, the place expanded until there were quite a few buildings spread over the many acres of fertile lands and fields.

I'd been corresponding with Catherine for a while and at some point felt led to ask her if guests were welcome at Combermere. She told me that the place was open to anyone who wanted to come and experience the life. I knew that she did not require that her followers take traditional vows of religious orders and that sounded really sensible to me. I talked to my Superiors about it and they graciously and unhesitatingly gave me permission to go.

The seven weeks I spent with this very loving, hard-working group of men and women was incredibly rewarding. We lived quite primitively; slept in large dorms on hard beds without even a curtain to separate us from one another: no privacy at all. We got up at the crack of dawn, lined up behind each other to have our chance at washing up at a sink, then hurried and dressed to get to the extremely beautiful Russian Orthodox Chapel to partake of the liturgy. There were no benches or seats to sit on, but we gladly remained standing throughout the whole service as we sang the soul-stirring Russian chants that lifted our hearts and minds to God. After the mass, we would silently make our way to the huge refectory where we sat eight people to a table and had breakfast, while Catherine read aloud from one of her books. When we were done we'd all go off to work to the place assigned to each of us that day. One of the neat things going on was that some of the priests chipped in for kitchen duty and did so very happily. It was a lovely sight seeing them scouring pots and pans and cheerfully greeting us as we passed through the scullery area. Now we're talking egalitarianism, I thought gleefully.

One of the beautiful men in the Community was scheduled to leave Combermere the following year, and showed an interest in me. His eyes and smile were pleasant to behold, but, regretfully, I was not ready to make a move in any direction, and so did not encourage him. Missed opportunity? Who knows.

Some of the Community members would get together for prayer meetings once in a while. I remember one time in particular when I had joined them, that one of the male participants spoke to me out of the blue and clearly stated, "*Vivian, you are very precious to the Father.*" I shook my head in firm denial, but he insisted, "*Yes, you are!*" I simply could not accept such singular attention and paid him no mind as I continued in silence and meditation with the group. I left the meeting as soon as it ended so as not to encounter him.

The same old fear pattern of coming off as special was in full swing here. Oddly enough, I actually enjoyed being the center of attention in a group, and always had some funny remark or tale to impart. I loved acting on stage, and in fact was quite at home there. Sticking out as exceptional or unusual in a spiritual sense was quite another matter though, which I was not willing to accept.

There were a few one-room cottages built on the grounds, far from the main buildings, called "poustinias." One could go there with a half loaf of bread, water, the Bible, a notebook and pen, and spend a night and a day in solitude in God's nature. I gladly took advantage of this opportunity and greedily drank in the sights and sounds that engulfed me and thirstily opened the holy Bible to hear the Word that God had for me in that moment, and every moment of that blessed day and night. I benefited from these private retreat days three times during my stay in Combermere, and the same recurring theme of *God as Father* came through every time I opened the Bible. I copied and treasured these lines, reading them regularly for many years.

As time went on, the ease with which I reconnected to the Father continued to grow and take on a life of its own. It became such that whenever I'd start to say the Lord's prayer,

I couldn't get beyond the words "Our Father," as a profound peace enveloped me and thoughts disappeared and stillness took over. I did not need any more words.

I remember feeling quite privileged to be able to go so quickly into deep meditation, thinking that no other member of my Community could pray this way. But one day I was taken aback and pleasantly surprised to overhear one of the Sisters, one that I'd never thought of as particularly spiritual, tell a group of Sisters around her that all she had to say was "Our Father" and she'd go into this profound meditative state. What an eye- opener that was for me! A good reminder to be more aware of my propensity to judge too harshly and too quickly. It is a tendency that is still part of my temperament and one of which I always have to be conscious.

My relationship with the Father grew healthy and strong again and stayed with me for many years. And then at some point, when I was back in the world, I started having doubts about the validity of my perception. Nobody talked of God as Father in my environment; God as Mother was in vogue. Was I imagining things? Was my devotion to Him simply a dream of mine? Once more I listened to my doubts, rather than to the quiet Voice within. Still believing my thoughts.

I'd been looking for a Community that was non-authoritarian, but I was not to find it at Combermere. I soon found out that the Baroness was anything but democratic. Quite the opposite, she was autocratic and dictatorial; she spoke, and people moved! Once during a meal in the refectory, Catherine yelled at one of the women in the room, "MILDRED!" The poor woman practically fell all over herself in an effort to answer the Baroness's call and attend to her in all meekness and submission. Horrors! This was definitely not the place for me. I loved the place, the chapel and the marvelous Russian chants, and the people who lived and worked there, and so I did stay the seven weeks allotted me. But as soon as my time was up, I gathered up my few belongings and returned to my convent, which at that time, was at least trying to make meaningful changes for the better, and for that I was grateful.

Another summer, I asked to take part in a venture where nuns from different Communities got together at a House of Prayer, so called because of the more contemplative life that was practiced there, in the hope of finding new meaning to the religious life they were living. The House that was chosen for the experience was in Gloucester, MA, on a Jesuit property located on the shores of the Atlantic Ocean. It was an awesome spot and had these immense flat rocks at the water's edge where we could stand and sit and breathe in the ocean's briny breezes and let the spray envelop us and refresh us. It was an ideal place for a five-week retreat experience. The schedule that we followed was structured, but left us enough time and space to wander outside to our heart's content. I actually experienced snorkeling for the first time in those clear blue waters. What an awesome privilege to visit this underwater world. I was totally impressed by the variegated colors of a domain that I'd never seen before, and I felt very blessed and very grateful to my Community for allowing me to continue on my search in this setting.

We rose early every morning to gather in a large room and sit on the floor opposite a picture window to feast our eyes on God's nature, while silently contemplating the beauty that greeted us. I remember an exquisite and huge spider web that had been spun in a corner of the window directly in the sun's path. It glowed in all the colors of the rainbow and evoked a touch of Fairyland. Nobody disturbed this enchanting, delicate spider-creation. It was such a gift, woven, it seemed, just for our pleasure and admiration and to enhance our daily meditation. We'd start the prayer time by chanting a Buddhist hymn of praise to God. We began the chant slowly and softly, keeping time with our hands beating the rhythm on our thighs, accelerating gradually to a resounding crescendo of joyous sound soaring with one voice of grateful praise reaching to the very throne of our Creator. Then we'd gradually decelerate the drumming and the chanting in a steady diminuendo until our voices became but whispers of adoration and love, gently coming down to an earthly landing in a hush of breathless stillness. The deep quiet and profound peace that filled us transported us into another realm which we were reluctant to leave. We'd stay in meditation for as long as we could, relishing every moment of this divine experience until it was time to go outside to celebrate Mass, where a huge rock overlooking the magnificent Atlantic became our altar. The entire ritual was transformed into a vessel of pure light containing the palpable Presence of a loving God who generously promised He would always be with us as we continued our respective journeys toward whatever kind of life was in store for us. There was nothing to fear.

A Jesuit priest, Father Peter, who had been with us from the beginning of our sojourn, made the celebration of daily Mass and communion possible for us. He was a beautiful young man who was also searching for his own path. He was non-threatening, gentle, kind, easy to talk with, and possessed a great sense of humor, so necessary for a life devoted to prayer. We couldn't ask for a more perfect environment for our search. We were truly blessed.

I must say that in spite of the beauty and the peaceful ambiance of the place, I was beginning to feel anxious and uneasy again. I'm pretty sure that my thoughts were at the bottom of the malaise I was experiencing. I simply was not aware then, that *negative feelings* are a sure indication that *negative thinking* is at play.

Sometime during the five weeks I spent there, a young man who was following the Buddhist tradition came to join us and lead us in five days of fasting and silent retreat. This presented no problem in itself, but came at a time when I was again really confused and in a particularly dark place.

One day during the retreat, I went out to the big rocks, and in my desolation I turned to God and cried: *"Father, give me a word!"* And again Spirit came through in a way I would never have expected: *Suddenly there was a thunderously deep Voice that came both from the heavens above and from the earth beneath my feet and slammed into my heart and said very distinctly: "YOU AND I ARE ONE!"* I was shocked and scared out of my wits! I ran from that place, just ran and ran. Who did I think I was that God would speak to me like that? I did not understand, and simply could not accept what had happened, just as I hadn't been able to accept being embraced by the Father as a young child, or being told that I was special to the Father. I felt baffled and mystified. Again I did not feel I could share this with anyone at the House of Prayer, therefore accepted the discomfort of the mystery, and put the incident on the back burner until the time came when I could get an answer from whomever.

Years later I heard these words again, put a little differently and in a much more gentle way. Upon awakening one morning, the words, *"The Father and I are One"* came to me, and my old resistance to being special reared its head. I thought, "This is blasphemous. It's all right for Jesus to say this… but me?" Nevertheless, a deep peaceful joy filled me, encompassed me, and comforted me for a couple of days. As I'd experienced before in similar revelations, my thoughts did not get in the way, and there was no more little me. I didn't understand what was happening but somehow the Father had taken over. It was absolutely awesome.

The next time this experience occurred, I was able to accept it more gratefully and gracefully, though I still did not comprehend it or know what I was meant to do with it. For a few days I walked filled with a sense of Presence enveloping me. Who could ask for anything more? I knew that the feeling would soon fade away and there was nothing I could do to prevent that. But unlike other times when I was left without any lasting effects, I discovered all I had to do to return to that special place was to say the words, *"The Father and I are One."* The words would resound in my being and I'd be thrust into profound peace. This happened at any time during the day, but especially at nighttime when I'd awaken; then I'd be filled with the Presence and swiftly go back to sleep. I still continue this practice every day and still experience as much calmness and deep quiet as ever, every time I say or think the words.

Cynthia Bourgeault in her book *The Wisdom Jesus* says that while Jesus claims that "the Father and I are one" (John 10:30)—*he does not see this as an exclusive privilege but as something shared by all human beings.* An amazing statement and one that I'd never heard proclaimed before. Personally, I am inclined to agree with her, even though this is such an unfathomable truth.

EMILY

Sometime during my stay at the House of Prayer, I met an extraordinary woman, the matriarch of an amazing family. I recall going to a prayer meeting at her house, where I felt immediately drawn to the remarkable energy that permeated the home and every one of its seven occupants. What a gift and eye-opener this encounter was for me. When I first saw Emily, I was first and foremost struck by her eyes: a luminous sky-blue that deeply radiated from the Light of her inner being. I gazed at all the five young boys and was amazed to behold the very same depth of Light and Essence emanating from each one of those lovely beings. When the father came home from work, lo and behold: the same illumination shone and spread out from him. What an incredible gift it was simply to be in their presence. Emily and I immediately connected, and before I left she invited me to come for an evening meal the following week. I gladly accepted, eager to immerse myself once more in their awesome energy.

We chatted while she was preparing the meal. I observed that she looked four or five months pregnant. She smiled, and clarified that she was not pregnant, but had some sort of illness which could not be cured medically. She was kept alive by the grace of God and was feeling really quite well. She then confided that she always felt Jesus's Presence with her. They walked together daily, hand in hand.

We sat around the long table to partake of our meal, and the youngest child, only five years old, read a few lines from Scripture as the blessing. It was so beautiful to see the joyful expression on everybody's face as he easily and clearly read the passage he'd opened to. Everyone listened with eyes closed and bowed head in deep respect and reverence.

The conversation during the meal was light and lively, and each one contributed and listened in turn. It was wonderful to sense the harmony and over-all delight they had in each other as they shared their day. I was deeply grateful to have had the opportunity to spend a little time with them. Their tangible joy and peace and love stayed with me for the remainder of my stay at the House of Prayer and for many weeks after.

I corresponded with Emily a few times after returning to the convent. In one of my letters I requested that she ask the Father what He thought of the Church. Her answer came a couple of weeks later. She'd had a vision, a dream. In it, she said that a lady went to visit a nearby convent and that the building looked quite forbidding. When the woman entered the convent, she was struck by the lack of color, the drab grayness of the hall and of the parlor to which she was led. A nun, dressed in a long gray habit, looked rather ill as she came in to give the woman a cup of tea. The lady accepted the tea but, as she went to take a sip she saw a huge spider floating on top of the beverage. She looked up at the nun who apparently did not even notice it. Then the nun told her that one of the sisters had died unexpectedly. They both went up the stairs to the sister's room. They found her lying down under the bed, mouth wide open, barely skin and bones. She had apparently died of starvation.

Emily went on to explain that the convent, the nuns, the grayness and dullness and lack of life were an allegory for the hierarchical Church which blindly starved its people by neglecting, ignoring, and misinterpreting the teachings of Jesus to satisfy a need for power, control, wealth and authoirtiarianism.

A hard interpretation, which, at that time, I was not convinced was entirely true. I had no idea that in the not-too-distant-future, I would be making a definite break from a Church that was way too autocratic and dehumanized, without feeling one iota of guilt or regret to stop or disturb me.

BREAKING FROM MY ORIGINAL COMMUNITY

All of these wonderful summer experiences happened between the time when I received the Baptism of the Spirit and the time that I found myself at the Christian Life Center, between 1969 and 1975. Then in the summer of '75, I accompanied a Sister who was attending a four-day conference in Virginia. Among the people who lectured I remember a Passionist priest, Father Richard, who spoke very clearly about the vagaries of Church leaders who were trying so desperately to close the windows that had been opened wide during Vatican II. He had been present in Rome during that historical period and had been highly encouraged to see that reforms were being put in place to start moving the Church in a new more Christ-like direction. Now he saw the refreshing results he'd been witness to being questioned and cast aside by the new pontiff and the curia: the papal court.

These old men who'd lived in the Vatican's palatial rooms for most of their lives, were utterly out of touch with the outside world and obviously regarded any kind of change as extremely threatening to their way of life and their autocratic rule. Certainly they were afraid that these changes would spell the end of the Church as they knew it. Whatever their reasons, gradually many of the hopeful alterations that had immediately followed the opening of the Vatican Council were eroded. Now that Pope John XXIII had safely passed away, the old guard was free to continue the traditional non-Christ-like way of leading the Church as they wanted. More's the pity.

I thanked God for the words coming from Father Richard and made an appointment to see him. We had a good initial conversation, and I asked if I could write to him. He gave me his address and I left encouraged by his words of wisdom.

After a few weeks back at the Center in northern Maine, I had quite a few talks with Sister Mary, the vocation director from Long Island, NY. After much pondering, I decided to write to Father Richard and express my concerns about the direction my Community was taking. In answer to my doubts, he wrote back and told me that if the Community was still hanging on to the practice of wearing a habit after all these years since Vatican II, they would never change. That was all I needed to hear to come to a decision. I also knew way down deep that if I didn't make the move then and there, I would never do it!

Why was making the change to go from wearing a habit to dressing as a lay person so important to me that it became the deciding motive for leaving my Community? Because I realized at some point, that wearing a distinctive set of clothes was profoundly and unequivocally symbolic of being someone *special*, someone *separate* from the rest of humankind, and way down deep that had become totally unacceptable to me.

After talking with Sister Mary, I felt confident I would be accepted into her Community once I let my own Superior know of my decision, obtain her permission to change Community, and contact the head of Sister Mary's Order to make my request.

I don't recall the whole gist of the conversation with my Provincial except that she gave me her consent readily enough, and in the next few days we started the process I needed to go through to move from one Community to the other. I believe that the Provincial and her council members had suspected for a while that I was on my way out of the Community and were probably relieved that I was finally coming to a decision.

In the fall of 1976, I was making my way from northern Maine to southern Maine to meet with the Provincial Superior when I realized that this year marked my twenty-fifth anniversary of taking vows with the Community. I was the last one left of the group of eighteen members who had entered with me in 1949. Of the three who'd taken final vows, one had died at age 45, and the other had left some years before. My departure spelled the end of that group. It pulled at my heart strings to be leaving, but I felt I was being led, so I did not allow worrisome thoughts to take hold of me. I determinedly pushed ahead into the unknown and, once more, confidently placed the workings of my life into the Father's loving and capable hands.

TO THE NEW COMMUNITY

The new Community was in Long Island, New York. The Sisters, known as the Daughters of Wisdom, had been dressing in lay garb for a long time. I fell right out of the habit easily and joyfully. Again, the four or five Sisters in the Community were very welcoming and kind, helping me to adjust to their very free way of living the religious life.

I was assigned to teach at Maryhaven, a school that took care of children who were emotionally disturbed or intellectually disabled. I soon fell in love with those kids. They were, for the most part, very sweet and beautifully innocent.

One day, I had just finished saying the opening prayer at the beginning of class, when Bonnie, a little child sitting at the rear, raised her hand. "Yes, Bonnie?" I asked. She piped up, *"Sister, your fly is open!"* Oh God, I felt like laughing. But those kids never laughed, not even the big boys. They seemed embarrassed for me and couldn't look me straight in the eyes. I pondered, as I sheepishly and smilingly zipped up, who would ever have thought that some day a child would find it necessary to say those words to a nun? I thanked Bonnie for her observation, smiled sedately at the unusually quiet class, and dove into the lesson as if nothing untoward had happened.

I spent two years with that Community. The Sisters were kind and patient with me and it was altogether a good experience, but I knew by the end of those twenty-four months that their way of living in Community was not what I was looking for. I did not feel that it was time to re-enter the world just yet, for I still had plenty of deep, personal cathartic work to do, though not in this Community. Besides, I had not yet received the sign to go back into the world, which I believed would appear when the time was right.

During my years in Long Island I was under the spiritual direction of a nun from another Community in the area. After two years of counseling with her, Sister Agnes knew me quite well and posed a question: Would I be interested in living a more contemplative way of life? If so, she had a place in mind for me; a cloistered Community that had made great strides in following the Vatican II guidelines. She knew the nuns personally and thought it might be a good match for me. Would I be willing to visit with them and assess the possibilities?

It didn't take me very long to decide to give it a shot. Was it possible that the yearning I'd felt for a contemplative life so many years ago was actually what God wanted for me? Since the opportunity to find out was presenting itself, I wasn't about to let it pass without looking into it.

Sister Agnes got in touch with the Prioress of the monastery and told her a little about my history. Having received the invitation to come and see, we both took off a couple of weeks later for the small village of Esopus in upstate New York, where the Community was located. The monastery was situated on the banks of the Hudson River on the grounds of a seminary for young men. The Redemptorist Fathers had inherited the beautiful grounds and vast impressive buildings from the previous owners who probably could no longer afford the huge taxes imposed on them. Donating the property to a religious institution was a good solution to their problem; this was a practice that happened quite frequently. The priests had then built a monastery on the grounds to house their counterparts, the Redemptoristine Nuns, who were the ascetic and contemplative half of the Order.

The monastery was a good sized building originally built to house fifty nuns. When Vatican II came around, Sisters who'd taken vows for life could be released from them if they felt, in good conscience, and for whatever reason, that they could no longer live that life. At the time of my visit most of the nuns (including the Mother Prioress) had returned to life in the world after the antiquated and suffocating religious rules spanning centuries had been relaxed.

When I visited the monastery, there were but eleven nuns left in the Community. Sister Agnes and I met with Mother Anita, the Prioress, and I was delighted by what I saw and heard and experienced during my short visit. She thought I would be a good candidate, and I was more than happy to take my chances. Mother Anita set the date for my entrance into the Redemptoristine Order in the fall of that year, and I gratefully set my sights on joining the Community at that time.

TO THE MONASTERY

In the year of Our Lord, one thousand nine hundred and seventy-eight, there went Sister Vivian (again) trotting off with her few belongings to yet another convent and another way of living in Community. I had great hopes that *This Was It!* It seemed very appropriate and fitting that this opportunity presented itself at this period of my life: the end was the beginning, so to speak.

The Sisters of the monastery were very warm and welcoming and seemed really pleased to have me join them. I was more than happy to know that there were three other recruits who had left their respective Communities to try out the contemplative life. We understood that it was a two-way street: we were checking the Sisters out, and they were observing and assessing us. It really was great having other Sisters as partners on the search and to know that I was not alone in learning the ropes of this new life.

The rules and regulations that we had to live by were quite different from non-contemplative Communities. Silence was strictly enforced unless it was really necessary to speak. We did not teach or nurse or go out of the monastery other than to take some fresh air. Our work consisted mainly in spending a few hours doing manual labor, and many hours in contemplative prayer, daily meditation, spiritual reading, the celebration of Mass, and reciting the Divine Office, a prayer observed by all monastic Orders in the world. This prayer took priority in our lives. We enthusiastic contemplatives-to-be embraced the life with all the zeal of new converts, getting accustomed to the many bells that called us to prayer, to work, to meals, to a meeting with the novice mistress for instructions, or to a study of the history of the Order. It was an exciting time and we dug in with bravado and much hope.

The Order was founded in the middle of the eighteenth century in France. The rules were written up by members of the clergy. This happened in all Communities, whether monastic or not. It was simply taken for granted that men wrote the laws that governed nuns' lives. And the rules were very tough, especially for contemplative Orders. Blind obedience was the order of the day, no exceptions. This meant no questions asked, no discussions, no excuses, ever. You either obeyed or you were advised to seek another type of Community. Thank God the days of unrelenting stoicism and medieval practices were long since gone by the time my friends and I entered the monastery.

As it was, the professed Sisters were all very glad to help us fresh recruits take our first halting steps in this revised version of the contemplative life. We had good times working together, singing together, and laughing a lot at our unavoidable missteps and mistakes. I loved Sunday evenings especially, when the hour of recreation was spent listening to wonderful music while playing cards.

However, I remember once blowing my top in exasperation while playing a particularly frustrating game, flinging the cards across the table, vocally expressing my disgust with a loud, "I'VE HAD IT WITH THIS STUPID GAME!" and heading towards the door, totally frazzled. How did the Sisters react? They did not reproach me or act shocked or scandalized at such infantile behavior, but laughed outright, loud and clear! That stopped me short, and I ended up laughing at my fulsome explosion as heartily as they did. What a marvelous and freeing experience. I could actually *be myself* in this Community! I felt that I'd stumbled into the kind of life I'd been looking for and it was nothing if not wonderful.

Though we dove in with much enthusiasm, the life was also stressful because it was so new and strange. As a means of relaxing I roamed the beautiful grounds and the nearby woods every hour that I could and harvested the variegated and luscious berries I found all over the bushes. Once I literally bumped into a deer looking for food among the same thickets I was investigating. I pulled back a branch and there was this big, beautiful animal with huge brown eyes right in my face. It was just as surprised as I was as we gazed for a moment into each other's eyes. Then, quick as a flash and silently as a cat, it turned and scooted away, creating but a tiny crackling sound of a breaking branch on its path. Astounding! What a treat. Berry picking had an even grander appeal for me after that wonderful incident. Thanks to the lesson learned from my father those many years before, I could not allow all this delicious fruit, literally at my fingertips, go to waste. It was such a joyous activity for me and I thoroughly enjoyed seeing the Sisters, who were not interested in picking berries, delight in eating them.

Nevertheless something was going on with me. I had a very difficult job to do. I was put in charge of the kitchen that very first year and I'd never cooked for a large number of people before. I tried to cook creatively, using recipes from books; I was told that I had to keep the meals very simple, the same as they'd always been. I obeyed without a moment's hesitation. Added to this, being the neat-nick Virgo that I am, I started cleaning out the equipment in the kitchen. I found that the back of the huge stove as well as the great big fan above the stove had never been cleaned. I attacked this carrier of grime-and-grease with enthusiasm and gusto. It took me several days to make the whole stove shine with a luster it hadn't seen since its inception into the kitchen many years back. It was beautiful. I was proud of the work I'd done, and totally exhausted. I started experiencing pain in my chest on a daily basis and finally confided in the Mother Prioress. I realized that I'd felt a lot of resentment at being left to do this herculean task by myself, however I never alluded to this in talking with the Prioress, (of course) but my attitude contributed to my distress. I eventually ended up seeing a heart specialist in the area whom the nuns knew and held in high esteem.

After listening to my story and to my heart he had me take a stress test, which I failed. He came back from poring over the test results and without a word, put nitroglycerine pills under my tongue. He said I might have angina and wanted me to take the pills every day for two weeks then come and see him again. I dutifully did this. He had me go through another stress test and once more I flunked. I was not surprised since I had not felt any change after taking the nitroglycerine. He became a little worried so he had me taken to the Westchester Medical Center by ambulance for additional testing. The medic in attendance said he'd never seen a heart patient look so calm and jovial. I knew way down deep that there was nothing physically wrong with me. I was just tired and stressed out; nothing to worry about as far as I was concerned.

After undergoing multiple tests during the week I spent at the Center, I was told that I'd passed all the tests with flying colors except for the stress test. My arteries were perfectly clear that they could see. Not passing the stress test was after all, a fluke.

I returned to the monastery with the same pain in my chest, though. That very day, I went to visit the female chiropractor who lived on the grounds. I'd had several adjustments from her, so she knew me. I told her what was going on and she looked at me in disbelief. Her reaction was a real eye-opener; *"Sister, what are you doing to yourself?"* I just looked at her, stunned. Then she put on a self-help tape. I listened to it, and when I left her, I used my day off to great advantage. While walking in the sunny outdoors, and breathing in the invigorating fresh air, I repeated these words from the tape out loud, *"I am well and healthy and strong, feeling fine and in perfect health, feeling better than ever before, without any pain in my body."* The pain gradually started lessening. By midday the pain was about half as bad, and, by the evening, the pain was gone. It was gone, and it never came back. I had felt all along that the culprit was the tension I was under. From then on with the heavy grueling physical work behind me, and by using the mantra as often as I needed to, the tension also lessened and I was able to continue being part of the Community.

An unexpected perk happened in my first year at the Monastery. For the first time ever, the Community allowed a Methodist minister, Mark, who was also a Jungian psychologist, to come and work with us. This was real progress, a genuine blessing, and a great opportunity. All but one of the Sisters joined the group: she didn't feel comfortable with the idea of baring her soul in front of the other Sisters. That was all right with the rest of us, and we soon started working with our dreams.

I can't remember most of the dreams that I recorded and after a while I discarded them because I felt they were all dealing with the past and had nothing to do with the present. But there is one that I remember vividly because it kept recurring even after I'd left the religious life.

I saw myself as a little child running outside in a beautiful carpeted field of wild flowers. With the sun shining brightly on my happy face, everything seemed idyllic except for one thing: there was a string extending from the house attached to my back. I could run just so far, then was pulled backward. I couldn't be free from the house!

To me the dream was saying that there was one "small thing" preventing me from living completely in inner freedom. There was obviously something from my childhood relating to my life at home that I had yet to come to grips with and resolve.

After I left the convent and with the help of friends that I trusted who'd had some training in counseling, I worked on my relationship with my mother, releasing deep feelings of anger and frustration and helplessness, and was finally able to forgive her, though I still did not trust her. When, a few years later, I went to visit her in the nursing home, (I was told by the person in charge, that she figuratively ruled the place in her own sweet and queenly way) I would imagine having a glass globe encircling my head, and see her words pinging off the glass, preventing anything she said from disturbing me. Then I could be gentle and caring to her, and listened to her for as long as she needed.

At some point, I stopped having the dream about being attached to the house in the field, and I knew that whatever that string had represented was gone. Something had been resolved and I was free.

The second year into the group therapy, four of the Sisters who'd participated stopped coming to the sessions. They found the work was getting too close to home, and that living in a cocoon environment made the sharing of their true feelings too difficult and unacceptable. We were now only eight participants; at the end of that second year, four others dropped out, so the Community abandoned the project altogether. It did not seem worthwhile to keep it up for only four Sisters. I was disappointed, and I asked permission to keep on with private sessions and was allowed to do so. God, I was blessed! I don't remember ever getting a "no" when asking any Superior to grant me what I deemed necessary and good for my well being. Was I spoiled? Yes, by God, I daresay.

I met with Mark regularly during the third year I was there, and also saw a priest of the Redemptorist Order for spiritual direction and consultation about what was going on in my life. They were both beautiful beings with whom I found it easy and helpful to talk, but as I look back now, I realize that it never entered my mind to speak about the mystical experiences and revelations I'd had through most of my life. Being burned by a priest once in my life had been one time too many.

Life was going along pretty smoothly and I was looking forward to pronouncing my solemn vows as a Redemptoristine nun in three months' time, when I would then be a member of the Community for the rest of my life. A major shift was about to occur, though I had no premonition whatsoever that it would happen so soon. I continued living my life as faithfully as I could as a member of the Community, doing the work assigned, finding sustenance and happiness in my prayer life, enjoying my interaction with my delightful Sister companions who were considerate, kind, and for the most part lived their lives with a gentle sense of humor.

PART THREE

WHAT'S REAL ANYWAY?

"I will betroth you to myself forever, betroth you with integrity and justice, with tenderness and love."
(Hosea 2: v.21)

A NEW BEGINNING

On July 3rd, 1981, I woke up in the middle of the night and suddenly *knew* in the depths of my being that it was time for me to move on, and move out, not only out of the monastery but from religious life altogether. There was no question about it, this was a message that resonated deeply in my heart. I realized that what I'd wanted to achieve before ever making the big step had come to be: I would be leaving without any bitterness and without any feeling of guilt, two feelings I'd successfully expunged from my life by that time. I was ready to go wherever the Lord would lead me and I trusted Him totally.

In order not to back down, I went to see the Mother Prioress first thing in the morning to tell her what had transpired during the night. She accepted my decision without question. I believe she and the other Sisters somehow knew that this day would come to pass. I was most grateful that they did not make it hard for me to leave. Every one of the nuns was supportive and very warm towards me. Soon after my decision was out in the open though, I felt a separation between us. I did not belong with them anymore.

Soon after, I had an appointment with Mark, the minister and psychologist that I'd been seeing for guidance. He told me that from the dreams I'd been having, he knew that sooner or later I'd leave the Community. He also said something that carried me through for many years. He told me, *"I want you to take it one step at a time. Not one day, but just one step. Can you do that?"* I said I thought I could. Of course, I was scared. I didn't know where I was going or what I was going to do. I didn't have any money, and I knew my family was not going to support me. But I never looked back and didn't dare look ahead. I remember telling God, *"Lord, I'm following Your lead. You'd better take care of me."* He did, and has, and still does.

Then I remembered a dream that I'd had many years before that was very relevant to my decision and which I'd experienced more than once through the years. In the dream, *I was in a room by myself. I walked to a door which I opened only to see complete darkness on the other side. I knew then, that some day I would have to go through that door, and that once I did, I would either step out on solid ground… or fly.* I felt I had just come to the door and opened it and I simply had to trust that the second part of the dream would also come to pass.

By what happened next and for years after, I can say that such has been the case.

EVERYTHING FALLS INTO PLACE

A year before I reached my decision, I'd read a two-year old article that an elderly nun in the Community at the monastery had placed on the table. It described the work of Therese Pfrimmer, a woman who'd found a way of curing the paralysis that left her unable to walk and which doctors had said was incurable. Therese was determined not to let this disability get the best of her. She started manipulating and massaging her legs using a method that she herself developed by separating adhered and fibrous muscles with her fingers and by working the deep muscles of her legs in a crosswise fashion. The deep tissue massage was very painful, but she did not let that stop her from massaging her limbs daily. In three months time, it paid off: she was walking again.

Since she did not know at the time exactly why her method worked, she furthered her study of massage and of the musculature system, and found that many health problems are caused by very tight, irritated, strained or unused muscles which inhibit the natural flow of blood coursing through the body. When she felt ready, she offered her services at a hospital for incurable diseases in the Toronto area. She used her own method of massage to help people suffering from multiple sclerosis, muscular dystrophy, parkinson's, arthritis, and other debilitating diseases and was rewarded with amazing results. The first patient she worked with, Edith, was in the last stages of an extremely bad case of M.S. Edith suffered from a swollen body and had not uttered a word in months; she could not eat and survived on drops of water placed in her mouth. Therese worked on her for four hours a day. At the end of three days, Edith said her first word. Therese had announced, "We're going to lick this," and Edith responded weakly but distinctly, "Yes." After three months of treatments, Edith was able to sit up in bed and do some exercises. She gradually was promoted to a walker, and a short while later, was walking down the halls pushing a chair ahead of her for support. After two years, Edith never had another treatment from Therese; she was released from the hospital and led a perfectly normal life for the next twenty-nine years. She passed away in 1976 at the age of eighty-two.

Therese started teaching her Deep Muscle Therapy method to others who were also interested in helping people regain their health. This simple method did not require the use of drugs, just dedication and hard work. She was soon offering classes in Canada and the U.S.A. and continued this work until she died.

When I read the article, I was touched to the core. This was something I wanted to do. There were Sisters in the Community who'd been suffering from arthritis for years and were getting progressively worse and I thought I'd like to help them if I could. I wrote to the people in charge of the clinic in Ontario and asked about their classes. They never wrote back and I thought that it simply was not meant to be for me. I did send the article to my mother who had arthritis to see if she was interested in looking into it. Later, I found that Therese had died shortly after the article had been written and things had changed in the organization. That was probably why I had not heard from them.

After my decision to leave the monastery was accepted by the Mother Prioress, I was given one week to travel to my hometown and break the news to my mother. I did not look forward to doing this at all. After the initial shock, Mom exclaimed, "But—I thought you were happy." How could I explain? I didn't have any words. She would simply have to accept that, after thirty-two years of living in Community, I was leaving religious life for good.

It was years before I found out that my mother never really accepted my decision. According to friends and relatives, she kept thinking of me and talking about me as "Sister Vivian." She couldn't let go of the illusion.

A few years later, when my mother died, I was asked to do a reading at her funeral. Although pale and shaken I did not shed a tear. Upon returning home, I was starting to give a massage to a client, when all of a sudden, I felt my mother at my side. She rolled up her sleeves, and looking at me with a great big smile said, "Let's get to work!" I knew then, that, at long last, she understood me and accepted me as I was, and probably helped me in my work more often than I was aware of... and, I'm sorry to say, more than I was willing to accept. I thought I had forgiven my mother; then I realized I still bore some resentment toward her. It was now my turn to ask her forgiveness, which I did, and felt better for doing so.

During the time I spent with Mom at home, she told me that she'd received a book written by a person in Ontario,

Canada, named Therese Pfrimmer. This was the same woman whose work I'd read about the previous year which had touched me so profoundly. The book was entitled *Muscles Your Invisible Bonds*. I enthusiastically read it, and suddenly the doors to my future were opened. In the back of the book, I found a letter to my mother indicating a person's name to contact in Deer Isle, Maine, and the phone number to call if she was interested in going for treatment, since Deer Isle is so much closer than Ontario. After thinking about it for a day, I decided to take a risk and call. I knew that the whole happenstance could not be just a coincidence. The Lord definitely had a hand in this! I had nothing to lose and was not about to let this incredible opportunity pass me by.

I called Deer Isle on a bright, sunny, Sunday afternoon. Diane, the person who answered, and I, talked for quite a while. She told me that she was giving her first class in about a month. Would I be interested in taking the class? I was, but remarked that I had no experience at all in this kind of work. "Well", she said, "come and take the class and find out if you have a knack for it. If you do, then you can pursue other studies in the same field as you need to. How about it?" I leapt at the chance, "All right, I'll do it!" I did not dare to consider where the money to take the course would come from or how I was going to get to Deer Isle or anything else. I was simply trusting, trusting, trusting, that it would all come out just right.

After a week at home, I returned to the Monastery to start proceedings for my departure, not only from this particular Community but from religious life altogether. I had to write a letter to the Bishop, then to the Pope, giving reasons for my request to be released from vows. That was easy enough, "*My mother made me promise . . .*" Then I had to let my original Community know about my decision. I did not care what the nuns thought or said about me. There was no question in my mind that this was something I simply *had* to do. No doubt about it.

A month or so later, permission had been granted by all parties concerned, and I received a request from my original Community to come to the Provincial House and sign the papers that would bring my thirty-two years of religious life to an end.

What did I feel? Some trepidation, some sorrow, but absolutely no guilt. I have never ever felt any guilt about the move, for which I am immensely grateful. I've heard of some ex-nuns who still carry guilt years after moving on. Not me.

The day of physically leaving the Community arrived. I had returned to the monastery to gather my few belongings and say my goodbyes to the Sisters, to my minister-counselor-friend, and to the priest who'd given me spiritual direction, who surprised me by getting teary. The Mother Prioress gave me three hundred dollars, which was all the Community could afford. It was not much, but they were poor, and I understood, and gratefully accepted what I was given. I went off with my sister, Rolande, and her husband, Roger, who had come to pick me up from New Hampshire to drive me over to some of my friends who lived in Massachusetts. Two weeks later, I turned fifty years old.

WHAT A ZANY WORLD!

My sister and brother-in-law dropped me off at the home of these two friends of mine, Meg, an ex-nun, and Betsy, who had been good friends since the time they'd worked side by side at the same home for emotionally disturbed children where I had lived and worked. They'd always told me to come to them when the time came for me to leave the convent, saying that they'd have a place for me.

I was supposed to stay two weeks at their chicken farm. I lasted one. Betsy was not a healthy person, either physically or emotionally. She had asthma and could not work at a regular job, so her parents had bought her this little chicken farm, in the hope that working out in the fresh air would be good for her. It wasn't. In her condition, working with the chickens was a handicap. She didn't last two minutes inside that coop. The ex-nun friend, Meg, who taught school, would come back after a hard day's work and go straight to the chicken pen to work. Betsy would go back into the house, get her inhaler, lie down on the couch, and breathe in oxygen until she recovered.

It was also evident that Betsy was not balanced. She'd throw tantrums at the least provocation. Losing a sock was enough to get her yelling at poor Meg, whom she'd blame for the smallest little mishap. She destroyed one of the big machines needed in her work for no reason at all and her screams of rage could be heard anywhere on the property. Meg would eventually succeed in calming her down, but it always took a large dose of cajoling and sweet-talking to do so.

I volunteered to help Meg. I worked hard and paid for my food, because their diet was a horrible mix of chips, hot dogs, twinkies, and coca cola! After Betsy found out that I had a little money, she charged me to stay there. I was flabbergasted! By the end of the first week, Betsy upset me to the point that I cried. That was the last straw. I moved out of there as fast as I could and found other friends to take me in. I'd lived and taught in the area for many years, so I did not have any difficulty finding somebody else to help me. I spent the second week with a really kind and undemanding family, which gave me a welcome break from the chaos of the chicken farm. Life in the outside world was proving to be no picnic.

Another of my sisters, Charlotte, also lived in NH. I went to spend the following week with her before going off for my classes in Deer Isle, ME. This likewise was a very difficult experience. My sister was a major alcoholic and so it was impossible to have a decent conversation with her. She'd sit in front of the TV with a glass of "iced tea" in her hand, while talking and crying incessantly. It was heartbreaking to see her destroying herself, but there was nothing I could do, except listen to her and love her as much as she'd let me. Apparently, I didn't succeed too well, because after I left she told my family that I never talked to her.

The following week, I was due to leave for Deer Isle for my course, but I had no transportation, and wondered how I would manage to get there. Again, the Spirit came through. A woman from Illinois, Sue, who'd been on a vacation in Russia, her native land, had contracted food poisoning while she was there.

She'd been due to take the Deep Muscle Course in February, but when she felt better and came back to Illinois earlier than planned, she called Diane to see if she could take the September course instead. Diane said, "Sure! And could you pick up this woman, Vivian, who is presently in New Hampshire, on your way here?" "Gladly," Sue responded. Problem solved, quickly and serendipidously. Now there was only the money to pay for it left hanging.

After I'd been to see my mother, I wrote to the Provincial of my original Community to tell her how I was doing and let her know about the course I would be taking. In the letter I mentioned the price of the course, but did not ask for any money. Some time before I left to go to Deer Isle, I had a dream in which I saw a check for the exact amount that I needed. A few days later, I received a check for that very amount from the Mother Provincial. This meant that I was able to take the classes without any financial stress whatsoever. What a blessing!

I have to say that I was really treated with much kindness by the Community with whom I'd spent twenty-five years. Later, after I'd started working, they also sent me a check for one thousand dollars. That was a lot of money to me! They wisely advised me not to touch this money, but to put it in savings and let it grow. I did exactly that, and later put it in CDs and then into mutual funds, all to my future advantage.

And so, towards the end of September, 1981, I rode off to Deer Isle with Sue to begin the course. We had a lovely time getting to know each other, talking about our very dissimilar, but adventurous lives. Sue was a wonderful person, and very dedicated to learning about alternative ways of dealing with aches and pains other than with drugs. From my sister's place in NH to our destination in Deer Isle, the trip took approximately five hours, but it went by very quickly when we discovered that we each had a wacky sense of humor;

and we often exploded in gales of laughter. We were both extremely enthusiastic about the course and the possibilities opening up for our future. It was an exhilarating time and we became fast friends.

Unfortunately, after some years of seeing each other at least every summer, I lost touch with Sue. It seems she became very ill, and her husband, for unknown reasons, stopped any possibility of my contacting her. I do not know if she is alive or dead, and I feel very sad about that, but there is nothing I can do. I know that she is in God's loving hands no matter where she is, and I am thankful to at least have known her and enjoyed her for a few years.

When we arrived at Diane's place, we met the only other participant, Joan. This was perfect, because being only three students meant each would get more needed attention and assistance. Part of the curriculum involved studying the different muscle groups, learning to work deeply in a crosswise fashion on tight and knotted muscles to release tension and pain, get the blood flowing throughout the whole body, and help restore the whole organism to vibrant health. We also spent some time studying kinesiology: learning to work with the energy around the body; reflexology: working on the feet which have reflex points to the whole body; and nutrition: learning about healthy foods that were also surprisingly tasty. There was much to learn. It seemed all we did was talk, walk, eat, and practice all that was offered to us every single minute of the day and into the evenings.

We all received a couple of massages from the two teachers, and learned the technique by massaging each other and offering free massages to the people of the area. I had much tension stored in my fifty-year-old-body, and when Diane gave me a first massage I thought, will there ever come a day when I will actually *enjoy* this? It was so painful! When I got off the table, I found that I could hardly walk, I was so dizzy and exhausted.

My malaise came from the many toxins that were released in my body from the massage. Still, it was a good hurt. I was more convinced than ever that this was what I *wanted* to do. And I knew when I first placed my hands on a human body to give a massage that this was what I was *meant* to do.

THE HOLISTIC CENTER

Meanwhile, there was a couple summering in Deer Isle that really appreciated my massages. They suggested that after the course I get in touch with the director of the new Holistic Center that was about to open in Portland, Maine, and ask if I could go for an interview. They would take me into their home for as long as was needed while I looked into things, in exchange for massaging their small daughter who had a spinal defect. I was so glad to take their kind and generous offer. They were so good to me.

After a couple of weeks of staying with them, my friends had found a place for me to live in the west end of Portland, a quiet residential area. I had a large room in the attic of a big, old brick house that sported a turret. It was within walking distance of many of the places I needed to go to for food and supplies. I went walking around Portland to acquaint myself with the library, the post office, the museum, and the shops. I loved this city!

My apartment was near a health food co-op, the Good Day Market, which was the first store of its kind ever, in Portland. I soon took advantage of the part-time work available there to earn the right to a 10% discount on what I bought. To my delight, the staff and management had a wealth of information which they gladly shared with anyone wanting to learn. It was there that I learned of the book *Sugar Blues*, which helped me change my life by inspiring me to give up my sugar addiction. Simply reading about how bad processed sugar is for the whole person was enough to turn me off of it forever. To this day, I still avoid processed sugar as much as I can, but at times find it hard to resist a tempting looking sweet. However, I mostly partake of the natural sugars like maple syrup, honey, etc. in moderation. From that initial exposure to healthy eating so soon after re-entering the world, I have been able to maintain good health throughout most of my life. I ate organically as much as possible but still shopped mostly at the big markets. At the time, they were much more within my meager budget.

That wonderful health food store eventually closed, but a husband and wife team, Lois and Dan Porta, who'd been instrumental in creating the comfortable ambiance of the place, built their own health food store in Scarborough Maine, called Lois' Natural Market Place, which is still thriving and very much appreciated by both locals and out-of-towners some twenty-plus years later. It is possible to get good information for whatever my body needs from Lois' and, as I continue to be mindful of what I put into my body, I am grateful their market is so close to home. Any doctor that I see is always amazed that the only medication I take is one baby aspirin a day. Besides eating healthy food and buying good supplements I do a series of exercises and walk the hills in my neighborhood every day. That's done the trick in keeping me healthy.

The director of the Holistic Center in Portland, was a physician. He was open-minded, kind, and willing to take on a rookie. I was advised to start looking for clients right away so as to begin working as soon as possible. With the help of some of the staff members who took me under their wing, I met the right person to help me do a bit of advertising. She created an attractive brochure and a lovely card announcing my work. She got them printed for me, and sent me off to different commercial places in the city to put them on counters and stick them on walls. The brochure was very well put together and got picked up wherever it was placed. Week after week I replaced the brochures that had been taken, but I never got a call from anyone. Apparently people liked the look of them, but only perused them, until finally one client who had seen and read the flyer, followed through by actually coming for a massage.

At that time, massage was a word that had a very negative connotation for most people in the area: they equated it with massage parlor, a place to be avoided. Therefore I talked to a lot of people, explained my work to them, and got my first clients that way. Having experienced how much better they felt from massage, they talked about it to their friends and relatives in need, and my clientele slowly grew. A chiropractor who had his office next to the Center bartered with me for as long as I was there. He was a big, gentle giant and he greatly appreciated and loved my work. We worked together on some of his more difficult patients who were hurting very badly. Our combined efforts brought good results, and he always said, "You don't need any more training. Just keep on doing what you're doing." Actually, I took many courses dealing with energy work, which was right down my alley, since I was very good at this way of healing.

Working at the Center, I was exposed to different gurus that were popular at the time. A few of the women with whom I associated were quite attracted to a few of these pundits and talked glowingly of them. I was never interested in finding out about their teachings or going to their gatherings. Christ and the Father were still very much in the forefront of my life. I was very leery of gurus and did not want to become involved in any kind of cult. Actually, becoming a nun had been 'cultish' enough for a lifetime! I define 'cultish' as any group that teaches that obedience is the number one law, for instance, taking precedence over love. I was fortunate that some of my friends were interested in getting together for a time of meditation, sharing, and healing every two or three weeks. This provided me with a sense of community and wonderful companionship for quite a few years. I was so blessed with my incredible friends!

One time, a renowned Reiki Master came to the Holistic Center to give a workshop. After the lesson, he opened up the session to anyone who wanted to be worked on. I don't remember if I volunteered, or if, having found out a bit about my background, he figured I could stand some healing. Anyway, I found myself on the table and experienced the hands of all my friends on my body. The dam broke and a flood of tears came rushing out. I didn't know what I was crying about; I just know I felt incredibly relieved and released from something that had been trapped inside my heart for a long time. The Reiki Master and friends kept their hands on me until I'd cried it all out, then gently hugged me one by one, whispering terms of endearment and encouragement as my sobs quieted down. What an experience that was! These caring people brought me much needed healing at that time.

Later, that same Reiki practitioner returned to the Center, for what seemed to be the express purpose of starting up a relationship with me. He did not approach me directly, but my friends did, and I declined. I was not ready for a relationship of any kind. Had I given up an opportunity to find a soul mate here? I'll never know. It just wasn't the right time for me. I felt I was in need of much more healing on the emotional level before I could open up to a liaison of this sort.

During my first summer out, though, I was approached by a man in a different setting altogether. I was working at a health resort northwest of Portland, giving massages and helping out with cleaning, doing dishes, and all the other things that needed doing in such a place. The staff was friendly, but I think some were into smoking pot, which I was not interested in trying. There was also a bit of philandering going on, which, (surprise, surprise!) I didn't care to try out either. But okay for them if that's what they were looking for.

Early one night as I was getting ready for bed in my little cubicle, my curtain door opened, and one of the staff members, dressed only in his bathrobe, softly padded into my domain! He thought perhaps to broaden my sexual education a bit. Give the little ex-nun the thrill of a lifetime? I looked at him with mouth wide open. I may have been naïve, not having even a passing grade in sexual schooling, but I was not totally dumb. Besides he wasn't even handsome. But handsome or not, that was certainly not the way I wanted to have my first romantic experience. I did not say a word but simply glared at him. He got the message and quietly and swiftly made his exit. He left disillusioned, no doubt, and justifiably so.

After one year of being affiliated with the Holistic Center, I decided to take the risk of striking out on my own. I had never gotten any clients through the Center, so I had no great incentive to continue working there. The staff people were very well-intentioned and well-meaning, but according to my observations through my year there, lacked some wisdom in the way they ran the organization. I could not imagine that the Center could survive for very long. Sure enough, a scant six years later it closed its doors, never to re-open.

When I left the Center, I also had to find another apartment. My landlady wanted the place to herself again. I was not sorry to leave, for I had often felt that I was back in the convent in that setting. I'd find notes she'd written complaining about one trifling thing after another. She was severe in her reprimands and was clearly not happy to have me in her house. Luckily, the same friends who'd found this apartment for me found another one (God bless them) again within walking distance of everything. It had a kitchen, a shower and toilet, and a small bedroom in the back. I ended up giving massages in the kitchen that year. During the winter, I'd open the oven door to get more heat while doing my work. My clients were non-complainers and took everything in stride, showing me only kindness and understanding. I don't think I can ever be too grateful for all the incredibly beautiful people that were always there for me whenever I needed them. Bless them all!

It took three or four years before my practice took off. I lived very frugally but had no complaints. People were very kind and generous. Many of my first clients became long-lasting friends with whom I still have a great and nourishing relationship. They generously gave me clothes, dishes, my first radio and tape recorder, a lawn mower, always providing me with things I really needed on birthdays and Christmas, always looking out for my welfare. I've been so very loved!!

Being on my own in a relatively big city took some getting used to. I'd entered the convent at eighteen, having lived all my life in a very small town in a very parochial setting, and led a very sheltered life. I really didn't have a clue about living in this totally new environment. Since I didn't have a car, I walked or took the bus everywhere (a great way to lose weight, I discovered). I'll never forget the first time I took the bus: I did not know the price of the fare, and instead of asking, I just put a quarter into the slot and walked to the back of the bus. "HEY!" yelled the driver, "THE PRICE IS THIRTY FIVE CENTS!" I very shamefacedly walked back to the front of the bus and deposited the extra dime, then sheepishly returned to my seat. Was my face red! I was totally embarrassed and flummoxed and told myself, next time *ask* when you don't know something, Viv.

Learning the ropes was surprisingly difficult for me. I remember thinking, I can't wait for a year to go by; things should definitely be easier by then. I did not have a license, therefore did not have any ID. That problem was brought home to me when I tried to open a checking account, "No ID? Sorry, ma'am, we can't help you." The bank didn't even want to take my money. Unbelievable; I was literally *nothing* in the eyes of the world. Being "nothing" was something that I felt somewhat at ease with, but, practically speaking, I couldn't live as a "nothing" on this planet. Oh my! Thankfully, getting my very own ID was taken care of a little later when a member of the Holistic Center in good standing with the bank, came with me for an interview, and vouched for my integrity and honesty, and *then* I was able to open an account. Another hurdle successfully dealt with. Again, thank God for friends.

A LONG TIME WISH COME TRUE

Since the time that I'd had the experience of looking into Jesus's eyes in the chapel all those years ago, I'd always looked for a picture of Jesus that would remind me of Him. One day, a psychologist friend of mine, Nancy, who was an admirer of Edgar Casey and had just returned from Virginia Beach where Casey's work is still going on, dropped in to see me. I had told her my story at some point, so she knew of my continuing devotion to Jesus. We talked a bit, then she said she had something to show me. She unrolled a large print, and as I stared at it my eyes opened wide; I gasped, and burst into tears. *The great Love coming from those eyes, the very same eyes that had so captivated me and healed me all those years before, were looking at me from this portrait!* (I remembered seeing a smaller black and white version of this picture in a magazine a few months earlier, and though I'd felt drawn to it, had ungraciously pooh-poohed it, "Nah! This couldn't be it.") Once again, Jesus reiterated clearly and powerfully that *His great Love was coming through for me.* My heart was pierced and filled with love to overflowing and I cried and cried and cried. My friend embraced me and held me close as she let me weep to my heart's content.

Nancy then shared how the portrait came to be: A beautiful young woman from Delaware, Nannette Crist, who had painted the portrait of several well known historical figures, was busily working on a painting of Benjamin Franklin one day when the picture of Christ came through. She'd painted Jesus's portrait before, so she attempted to paint the historical figure a second and a third time, without success. Finally, she realized that she was being directed to paint Christ's portrait once more. As soon as she started working on the canvas, *Jesus appeared to her and stood beside the easel for the length of time it took her to do the portrait.* She spent three days and three nights working without food or sleep to complete the painting. When she finished, Jesus said to her, *"This is to give to those who love me."*

The artist then sold a print of the portrait to the Casey foundation and they advertised it in their magazine. Because I was so deeply touched by the picture, and after I'd stopped crying, my generous and kind friend gifted me with the beautiful twenty-four-by-eighteen inch copy that she purchased from Nanette. I value it more than anything else I have in my home, except for my kitty cat, Elmer, of course!

The very next day I received an additional gift. A young friend of mine dropped by my house to see me, and I showed him the picture that was still bringing me to tears. He was very moved by it and offered to frame it for me. A few days later he came back with the framed portrait. The frame was beautifully and artistically done with smooth blond wood, and the matting was a perfect match for the colors that the artist had used. I hung it on my living room wall so that my friends and clients could easily see it. Many were brought to tears when gazing upon it, while a few, for some strange reason, could not bear to look on it. As for myself, for many years the portrait was the focal point of my meditation. I would look into those loving eyes until my mind quieted and I found peace and joy again. It was the most healing, life-giving present I ever received and I benefited from it for a very long time.

Then one day, years into the experience, I decided it was time to stop using the picture in that way because I was having doubts about the whole experience. I had learned that one was supposed to find answers within, not look to someone outside oneself for solutions. Wasn't Jesus outside of me? How could a picture give out so much energy? I was listening to my mind and my fears again and for a long while deprived myself of the loving comfort and help that had been my lot for such a wondrous period of time.

I've since come to realize that it's not necessary to understand everything, but simply accept and be grateful for whatever way I sense the Presence. Adyashanti, who trained as a Zen Buddhist monk and who is a very wise spiritual teacher, says that Zen Buddhists have many pictures of saints on their walls, and believe that gazing upon any one of them over a period of time will eventually render the observer to be like the one gazed upon. Not a bad idea after all, since the holy one's energy is actually coming through, because, as it's becoming ever so much clearer to me, we, and everything else, are all made of energy: the electro-magnetic energy of love.

And so, I once more gaze upon Jesus's portrait, which now hangs in my bedroom, and allow His Love to flow through me. Besides, looking at Jesus's portrait is the same as gazing on a favorite picture of a beloved person who's passed away, which everyone does quite naturally.

Divine Presence fills me
Unconditional Love envelops me
I, and all beings, are loved beyond compare

THE PRESENCE IS EVERYWHERE

After I'd been living in the world for a couple of years, I woke up one Sunday morning asking myself why I was going to Church. The only thing that drew me was the Eucharist (The sharing of the bread and wine as Jesus shared with his disciples when he said: *"This is my body, this is my blood."*) I decided then and there that it was time for me to break away from a Church that did not make sense to me anymore.

Some time after I took that step, I had a revelation. I was sitting in my living room, meditating quietly, when I heard the words, *"Everything in nature reveals the Presence of God."* The words were spoken softly and gently, but held tremendous power and authenticity. I looked at my surroundings: my pleasant sun-lit room with its plain but homey couch, rocking chair, recliner, attractive wooden floor, my picture window providing me with a beautiful view of trees near and far, exquisite sunrises, breathtaking seasonal thunderstorms and snow-storms, and I thought, *"Yes! This is It."* God is not only in the Eucharistic Presence, He is everywhere. All I have to do is look around me and behind the material world to see the Divine Presence in me and in everyone and everything I see.

This does not mean that I never partake of the Eucharist anymore. When the occasion presents itself, I gladly and respectfully take the sacrament at wherever church I may happen to be, for I do not believe the Eucharist is the exclusive gift of the Catholic church, but of any church that offers it.

Recently, in a book by Cynthia Bourgeault, *The Meaning of Mary Magdalene*, she tells of her partner asking his brother at one point, "Why do you believe in God"? His brother answered. *"Look around you."* And her partner looked and looked and looked until he saw the Presence of God everywhere… and his life was changed forever. Pretty powerful.

Doing what I thought was right for myself (such as leaving the church) without consulting any authority figure was a huge change for me. True, I was sure for a very long time that I was where I was supposed to be. Then, at the age of thirty-nine, after being exposed to the Charismatic movement and to the reality that I did not have to be a nun to be close to God, I finally started thinking for myself. That's when the fun began! I had been under other people's domination long enough. It was high time for a change.

Once, as a nun, I happened to be in the midst of a group of priests who had served in my parish when I was growing up. I was shocked beyond belief to hear one of the most respected priests of that era talk and laugh about the simple faith of the people of my hometown. He talked freely about the gullibility of these people right in front of me. I was appalled and angry: How could he be so heartless and arrogant?

Keeping parishioners uninformed or misinformed was, I gathered, common practice among some members of the hierarchical Roman Catholic Church in order to keep them under their clerical thumbs. Was this what Jesus the Christ meant when He commissioned His disciples to spread the good news of God's eternal, undying Love for His people? When He preached about the two commandments of the new covenant: *"Thou shalt love the Lord thy God with thy whole heart, and mind, and soul, and thy neighbor as thyself."* Or when, surrounded by little children he said: *"What you do to the <u>least</u> of mine, you do to me."* It seems to me that many of the clergy have missed the mark and are sorely in need of taking a good look at themselves and at what they preach and how they live the Gospel. They deeply need to modify the way they deal with the people whom they are supposed to serve. I remember one priest who boasted about his life as a member of the clergy: "We've got it made!" he said, "I've got a nice car, have wonderful free vacations, and people love me and give me all sorts of presents! What a great life!" He was a good man, simply pretty unconscious and unaware.

This is not to say that there are no beautiful and holy people in the convents and churches. There are those who stay connected because they have a real calling and feel they're more capable of bringing about change from the inside than from the outside. If this is what their hearts tell them to do, then God bless them, for theirs is a difficult path. I was meant to do otherwise. This is where I'm at, and this is where I'm happy to be. I am relating to God in my own way and am at peace with myself.

LEARNING TO DRIVE AND BUYING A HOUSE

After being part of the Portland scene for five years, I decided it was time to learn to drive. When I called a company to get Driver's Ed lessons, the man asked me how old I was. When I said, fifty-five, I was taken aback by his response: "Why are you learning to drive at *age fifty-five?*" Fifty-five is not that old, I thought; what's the matter with this guy? Anyway, In spite of his negative attitude I got my license, and greatly enjoyed the freedom that driving that old car gave me.

As soon as I had a chance, I bravely went by myself to New Hampshire to visit my sister, Rolande, and her husband, Roger. They'd given me directions but weren't very specific. Being a new driver I *needed* specifics. The first year I attempted to get to their house, I phoned them from a place probably ten miles away. My brother-in-law came to get me. The second year, I phoned when I was a little closer to their home. Again Roger rescued me. The third year, I got much closer, but still had to call him for help. Finally, the fourth year, I actually landed at their door. What a sense of triumph and accomplishment! It took me a little while, but so what. My sister and brother-in-law were duly impressed.

I was amazed at how much independence I derived from being able to drive. No more wasting time waiting for a bus, no more calling on others to go somewhere I wanted to go. I was my own boss and enjoyed my liberty as much as any teenager.

My sixth year in the Portland area, I was going to have to move for a seventh time. My landlords, who were friends of mine, had forgotten to inform me that they'd had plans to sell the house from the onset of my moving in. I was *not* going to move into another apartment, so the only alternative was to buy a house. I'd never thought of doing such a thing. I had no money, and the thought of maintaining a house, with all the responsibility that came with it was enough to daunt a hardier spirit than mine, for a while. Then I became determined to go ahead as if I didn't have any money problems and started looking into possibilities.

I thought about the thousand dollars I had been given by my original Community the first year after I'd left the convent. The Provincial had told me not to use it, but to put it into savings. I'd done that, then found that CDs were more profitable, and later moved the money into a mutual fund which was even more profitable. At some point, somebody told me about a company called A.L. Williams, which dealt only in mutual funds. A representative contacted me, and convinced me that I would benefit much more by taking a mutual fund with *his* company. So I moved my money, about $5000 at the time, from my bank into the A.L. Williams Co. The monies grew for a couple more years, and when I looked into how much I'd have available to buy a house, I was pleasantly surprised to find that my assets had grown to $10,000! Amazing! I was going to go ahead with the plan, for I felt it could become a reality.

I then contacted a former client of mine, Sally, who was in real estate. She told me the first thing to do was to buy a daily paper (something I never did), and look at the ads for houses every morning. OK, I could do that. The next day, I got a paper and looked at the houses that were advertised. They were all more expensive than I thought they would be. The price for the type of house I was looking for had gone up from $60,000 to $80,000 in just two weeks' time.

One house caught my eye, and I called up Sally and brought her attention to it. We decided to go look at it that very day. The house was located near Veterans' Bridge, which spans the Fore river between Portland and South Portland. When I first saw it sitting on a hillside, with a great, big horse chestnut tree in full bloom on the front lawn, my heart felt a quiver of hope and excitement. I'd had a dream of a house sitting on a hillside looking very much like it a few nights earlier. An elderly couple had been the only owners of the house and were looking to sell for their retirement. The backyard was all overgrown bushes but I figured that could be remedied in time. The interior would need some cosmetic work, but I saw the potential for aesthetic changes all over the place. It was perfect for what I needed, and I was told that the builder had been one of the best in the area, and that it was only twenty years old. The couple had not had any previous offers for the house, since this was the first day it was on the market, and I told them that I was definitely interested and would start negotiations right away.

The next step of course, was finding a bank that would be willing to give me a loan. Suddenly, $10,000 seemed very modest. I was not too surprised to find out that no bank was willing to take a chance with me. I really had very little income to work with, which my income tax return would quickly reveal.

My friend said there was one more bank we could go to. This bank was willing to bypass scrutinizing a person's income tax return, if said person could come up with 25% of the cost for the house up front. In this instance that meant paying $20,000 right off the bat. Oh my, what to do?

Then I remembered my sister, Rolande, and her husband, Roger. I had some connections and I was not averse to asking them for help.

This was a little difficult, for they both had health issues at the time and all communication was done by phone as they were in their Florida home. I talked with my sister, who was very kind-hearted, who talked with her husband, who was a man of business. We hung up, and I left it in the Father's hands. If it was meant to be, it would happen; if not, then that would be for the best, too, I was certain of that. The process went on for two or three more phone calls over a period of a couple of weeks, during which time they always gave me a pretty favorable response. I held my breath.

Then one day they called to tell me their decision. They would help me if I was willing to pay them 8% interest. I was tickled pink. God bless them! Their willingness to take a chance on me proved that this purchase was indeed meant to be. Even though this would add to the mortgage interest and felt a little overwhelming, I put all worry aside and went for it. I am pleased to say that I never missed a payment, a miracle in itself, and when Roger passed away, my sister graciously forgave the money I still owed. She really was a love.

I signed up and became a bona-fide home-owner with a 30-year mortgage. Pretty scary stuff, but I've never regretted it. And later, when rents soared higher and higher, I had ample reasons to be grateful for following my heart.

Shortly after I bought the house, the country went into an economic recession. The agent from A.L. Williams who'd been responsible for helping me accumulate a respectable sum from that mutual fund, told me that I'd bought the house in the nick of time. If I hadn't done so, I would have lost everything! Certainly Somebody was looking out for me.

Many years later I found out that everybody in my family thought I was crazy to buy a house and at such a price! Well, maybe I was a little bit nuts, but they'd also thought that about me when I'd left the convent six years earlier. "Leaving all that security, oh my, she's got to be off her rocker." A few years later their negative attitude changed to a cautious pride for what I'd been able to achieve; at times they even talked of me in glowing terms. A lovely new approach.

Many of my wonderful, caring, friends gladly came to my assistance to help me put my house in order: I had a friend who cleaned out the oven and confided that she never did this work in her own house, but happily and generously did it for me. Three of the nuns who had been my companions in the monastery a few years before and who had returned to their original Communities, traveled from their respective convents in New Jersey and Massachusetts to come to my aid. They were such darlings, and we had such a good time, working assiduously at our tasks, but taking much needed breaks for relaxation on whatever comfy surface we could find in the little house. We laughed while remembering stories of life in the Monastery and caught up with each other's doings since those never-to-be-forgotten days.

My dear friends left after a few days, traveling together to their respective convents. I sent them off with great gratitude and deep love. I never saw them again, but still keep in touch with two of them, and remember them as being the best of the best.

I have now been in the house for over twenty-seven years and have grown to love it more and more for perks that I wasn't even aware of when I bought it. It is in a perfect location: I am just five minutes from anywhere in Portland; the highway is right around the corner; the airport about ten minutes away; and the beaches are a distance of about six miles. In short I have easy access to everything, and my lovely backyard is ideal for gatherings and birthday parties.

Without the help of my many friends, women and men, I would never have been able to clear out overgrown bushes on my grounds, plant lilacs and trees, and have beautiful gardens growing year after year in my big backyard. I am truly and incredibly blessed with all the really wondrous people in my life.

I must say that I also have great neighbors who are friendly, accessible and helpful. Whenever I'm away for a few days, my precious cat, Elmer, is lovingly taken care of in the mornings by Toni across the street, and in the evenings, by Corey, living on my left, or Ed and Heather, living on my right. Bob, across the street generously snow-blows my driveway in the winter, and his grandson, Antonio, mows my lawn in the summer. I couldn't ask for better neighbors! Through all these years the blessings have kept coming at the right time for me, without my ever having to ask for them.

A SHORT TERM RELATIONSHIP

My life was going along pretty smoothly, but something kept cropping up that I felt needed looking into. Was it time to seriously look for a soul mate? How could I go about finding one? I started perusing one of the free local papers that had ads for women seeking men. I answered a few of them over time and met one or two men over lunch. Nothing clicked. I went with friends to singles dances every once in a while but had no positive outcome. The first time I went, though, I was dancing with a man, and casually (and mischievously) mentioned that I was a former nun. He backed off as if I was dangerous material! During the remainder of the evening I saw him turning away from me whenever he chanced to be in my line of vision; the man was really scared. He must have been a Catholic. No Protestant would have been so petrified at the mere mention of my prior life. In fact, other men that I met were at first surprised when I brought up the subject, then became interested in hearing my story. Needless to say, I became a little more circumspect in giving out that bit of information after that man's fearful reaction.

During my second year out in the world, two of my women friends who lived in a beautiful place close to the beach, offered a weekend workshop entitled Union With God. This sounded great to me, and I signed up. Among the participants in the workshop were a couple of men, one of whom was older, probably in his sixties, who looked very kind and seemed interested in me. I thought that being at this meeting probably indicated that he was interested in some sort of spirituality. Why not give it a try? I encouraged his advances, and soon we were talking, laughing, and taking walks. Then I invited him to my place for an overnight stay.

Fred was gentle, patient and kind with me as I had my first experience making love. After it was over though, I remember thinking, "Is *this* what the big fuss is all about?" It wasn't even pleasurable. And *this* is supposed to be a mortal sin? You've got to be kidding! I could not help but compare the relatively so-so feeling of this sexual encounter to the unbelievably exquisite experience of God's Love that had filled me years before as a young twenty-three year old nun. And I was convinced anew that for as long as I drew breath, nothing, *nothing,* would ever come close to the ecstasy I felt on that memorable day. Nevertheless, being human, I did have a few more encounters with him.

On one of these visits, we were lying down side by side on his bed, fully dressed. He wanted to share one of his writings with me. I lay down comfortably in the crook of his arm and he started reading. At one point, he turned to me to ask a question, which woke me up. He was incredibly insulted and rattled, *"You fell asleep!?"* "Guilty", I replied. He couldn't believe it. I had dealt him quite a blow. I felt like laughing, but didn't. Then one day I found out through his own admission that he believed it was perfectly fine for a man to have relationships with different women at the same time in order to satisfy his needs: his sexual needs, his intellectual needs, his culinary needs, and so on. I didn't need to hear any more of his quirky philosophy before dropping him. I did not resume my quest for a soul mate for a very long time after that experience.

THE UPS AND DOWNS OF SPIRITUAL GROWTH

Right through the 1980s I continued dealing with my thoughts as I'd done for many years while in the convent, that is, controlling them, then eventually dismissing them altogether by not paying attention to them. I was actually on a spiritual and emotional high for several years. I felt free and liberated. I often danced for joy in my living room and was full of love for everyone. I sang songs of praise and thanks at gatherings with friends, and was literally bubbling over with enthusiasm for the Lord and His Love for me and His Creation.

There was a thought that kept nagging at me, though. I'd heard and read that one was supposed to look and examine the thoughts that appeared in one's head. In my understanding, that meant paying attention to them, which I'd resisted doing for years. The way I'd been handling my unwanted thoughts had worked very well for me, so why do it differently? My problem was that I still did not trust my intuition on the spiritual path, and, not knowing any better at the time, I gave in to the thought that I needed to *examine* my thoughts. As soon as I made that choice, I felt as if I were wrapped in a heavy, dark pall. I became downhearted in a way I hadn't been in a long, long time. Joy, which I had always been able to return to, no matter what, was still there in the depths, but decidedly buried.

For several years I plodded along miserably, hating myself for doing this to myself. It was strange but even though I knew I was causing the problem, I couldn't stop myself. I had developed a very debilitating habit.

Just the other night, all these years later, I suddenly came to the realization that the feeling of gloom that came over me with the decision to examine my thoughts, was due to the fact that I had felt somehow disconnected from God, the One who meant *everything* to me, my Life, my Love, my All. I, who had heretofore gone straight to my center with my breath and sensed my God there, and by simply saying the word "Father" was always able to return to equanimity, had now cut myself off from that wondrous available Source of peace and joy. I felt I did not deserve God's love anymore, and I felt saddened beyond belief. This was an incredibly difficult period in my life. I needed help, and God provided in the following way:

I opened myself up to new teachings, which helped me find my balance again and arrive at exciting new realizations and possibilities in my pursuit of spiritual growth and spiritual freedom.

In 1999, I accompanied my psychic and spiritual friend, Ann, to a retreat place in the Blue Hills of Virginia for a week spent immersing ourselves in the loving, peaceful environment of an idyllic spot on Mother Earth. The minute I set foot on the grounds I felt a deep calm envelop me, along with a profound feeling of being loved. The men and women who made up the staff were very kind, thoughtful, and loving, and I quickly felt at home and at ease with them and my surroundings. I did not have the means to pay for both the trip and my stay at the Center, so the retreat master allowed me to participate in the program in exchange for manual labor. I took advantage of this offer seven times over a period of three years. This worked out fine with me and gave me the chance to make meaningful changes in the way I lived my interior life.

The retreat master, affectionately known as M.C., who spoke to us every evening, inspired me with words I needed to hear again, *"Thoughts are not important. Living in the present moment, in the here and now, is the only way to live. Do not let one precious moment go to waste!"* Using the mantras: "Thoughts are not important" and "Here and Now," I found myself able to let go of negative thoughts, stay in the moment, and reconnect to the Presence within once more.

Little by little as I repeated the mantras over and over during the week I spent there I began healing at a deep level. I started to feel the deep peace and joy "that surpasses understanding" come alive in my whole being once more, much to my delight and relief.

To help me go to sleep one night when I was back home after the retreat, I said the mantra "Now" repeatedly until I dropped off peacefully. One night, the method was not working very well, and I was getting really restless, when, out of the blue, these words arose in me, loud and clear, "THE ETERNAL NOW!" The words seemed to flow into my left arm, which I'd flung to the side, and enter my heart easily and quickly. They were a soothing and restful balm for my soul. Any thoughts trying to invade my mind were quickly dissipated by repeating them, and sleep promptly followed. I was thoroughly overjoyed and deeply grateful for this new mantra which I used successfully for many, many months.

For years, I've used different methods to help me when I wake up at night and worry about not being able to fall asleep again. One night I simply stopped *believing the thought* that I wouldn't go back to sleep; I focused on my breath, got very quiet, centered on the divinity within, and quickly dropped into deep sleep. Often what has worked for me is simply saying or thinking the name "Father" or "Jesus." At one point I realized that worrying reveals that I am not living in the present, so saying the word "Now" or "Eternal Now" or "Right Here, Right Now" is right on. This empties the mind of noisy thoughts which allows sleep to come naturally and easily. Other times, I put myself aside, stop thinking about myself, and focus on sending love to others.

During my next retreat at the center in Virginia, I shared my practice of saying *"The Eternal Now,"* with a fellow participant, Patrick, who had become a good friend. His reaction was, *"That is God!"* The remark stunned me and took me aback. I did not understand or really take in what he said, but I continued the practice anyway, because it felt so good and somehow so right-on.

I presently understand that the "Eternal Now" is but another Name for God, along with "Source," "Presence," "Being," "Consciousness," "Spirit," "Love," "Father," and so many other Names, depending on one's cultural and religious upbringing. So many different ways of connecting to the Divinity within, all perfectly agreeable and acceptable to the One Essence beyond all physical life.

Upon returning home after each of the retreats I made, the euphoric feeling I'd felt would last for about a month, and then it was back to the grind. However, there was an added dimension to my struggle: I had tools to help me stay centered. I repeated mantras to help me stay in the present moment throughout the day. *I could do this!* And my renewed focus was sensed by my clients. One told me while I was massaging her that she always felt tremendous peace during the massage. Another dear person said that she came regularly for massage to help her keep her sanity. I was thrilled, and realized that yes! way down deep, peace and joy had returned full blast and had again become an ongoing blessed reality in my daily life.

GOD LIVES IN THE EVER PRESENT MOMENT

Many years ago I started working with my dreams and keeping track of them. One dream that I still remember vividly because of the message within it, and because I've tried to implement it ever since, is this one:

I was in a museum and was facing a wall on which a panoramic view of a magnificent estate was portrayed. A lovely white house with red trim and gabled roof sat on the highest peak of a hillside; lawns spread like velvet in undulating waves of green, shimmering in the sunlight across the entire landscape. Most amazing of all were the incredibly beautiful roses of every color and hue that meandered downward from the facade of the house and on either side of a walk to the path below. As I was gazing open-mouthed at this wondrous sight, suddenly the roses changed appearance. They were in the same setting but showed up in all different sizes and colors. This happened again—and again—and again. Incredibly, each scene was even more beautiful than the last. Then the thought came to me, this can't be happening. I must be going crazy. And then, oh well, so what. I'm just going to enjoy it… And I woke up.

I knew there was a hidden meaning in this dream, and that if I went back to sleep I'd get the answer, so I did, and re-awakened to these words, *"God lives in the ever present moment, so must you."* I agreed wholeheartedly, but thought, "OK—but how do I *do* that?" I could stay in the present for a little while, but thoughts about the past or the future would get a hold of me before I even realized what was going on and I'd find myself trapped in a quagmire of my own creation. I had recourse to different mantras to help me get back into the moment such as: *"Now!"* or *"Now is where God Is!"* And those would work for a time, then I'd find myself in a stuck place again. Once I wrote a little ditty extolling the necessity of staying in the Now and sang it over and over:

> *This is the moment, the only moment*
> *Now is the only reality*
> *Live in the moment Enjoy the moment*
> *It's all you have, you see!*
> *The Past and Future are both resolved*
> *By living in the Present*
> *If you want bliss remember this*
> *Live fully in the Now! (ref.)*

I soon realized that I was not the only one having trouble living in the present. It was difficult for everybody.

In 2001, I came across Eckhart Tolle's book, *The Power of Now* and the works of so many other wise spiritual leaders who were all teaching about the importance of living in the moment. Since God lives only in the present moment, it simply makes sense that the *Now* is where we find Him—Spirit, Source, Presence, God, Father—whatever you may call It, is really leading us back to the moment. People are becoming more and more aware and waking up to a new consciousness: God is here, right here, right now, no doubt about it. And, as Eckhart says, *"You can always come back to the Now."* Wonderful! Again, thoughts that are about the past and future are just thoughts; they are ephemeral and have no reality—why allow them to run our lives?

Eckhart continues: "You are not your thoughts. Thoughts are nothing, feelings are nothing, and the body is nothing." Everything that has form is but a manifestation of the Formless, meaning: God is the Only Reality. *"One way that you can learn to return your attention to the timeless present moment is to become aware of your breathing for it takes attention away from thinking and creates space. When you are present, when your attention is fully in the Now, Presence will flow into you and transform what you do."* Focusing on my breath is an easy way for me to come back to the present throughout the day when I suddenly realize I'm somewhere in the past or in the future.

Adyashanti, who loves the Christ and is not affiliated with any religion, gave a teaching on living in the present which I think, says it all:

In this moment, there is always freedom and there is always peace.
This moment in which you experience stillness is every moment.
Don't let the mind seduce you into the past or future.
Stay in the moment, and dare to consider that you can be free NOW.

He also teaches that we don't need to strive for perfection but simply accept ourselves as we are in each moment no matter what we're experiencing or feeling or what thoughts are going through our minds. I have learned to make a practice of saying these very powerful and healing words: *"It's OK, it's all right, it is what it is, it's just a thought, it's just a feeling.*" No thoughts or feelings are right or wrong in themselves. They are not ours to begin with, but I believe come from the collective consciousness all around us. It is up to me to make the choice of whether to let go of the thought or feeling, or not.

I've often experienced the power of staying in the Now, but never more so than last week, when, while driving in the right lane leading to an intersection, a car coming from the opposite direction was heading straight into me! We both stopped *inches* from each other; I felt fear and anxiety building up as I resumed driving; then, these words came to me, "*That's in the past... Let it go.*" I stopped thinking about it, and blessed calm returned to my being once more and I peacefully resumed driving. I've been using this method regularly since this almost-accident happened: I suddenly become aware that I'm thinking either of the *past* or of the *future* and as soon as I realize it I simply say "It's in the past... let it go." "It's in the future... let it go." And it works. Even if an event is just a second away, it's in the past, and one can easily let go if one recognizes it for what it is: *something that's already gone by and has nothing to do with the Now.* Letting go of the future means that one does not ever dwell on "*what ifs...*" which are totally useless and debilitating. *If you want bliss, remember this, live fully in the now.*

And then I became aware of Byron Katie's book *Loving What Is,* in which she helps people confront their thoughts with these three questions: *Is it true? Is it absolutely true? Who would you be without that thought?* And then she says to *Turn the thought around.* A very helpful and practical process. I read her book and diligently asked the question "Is it true?" every time a thought came up that felt negative. If I found the answer to be "Yes." I would then ask further, "Is it absolutely true?"

Inevitably the answer was "No." (There are very few thoughts that are absolutely true*)*. Then I would proceed with the next two steps. Turning the thought around proved to be the more demanding step. For instance if I think: *"My mother doesn't love me,"* turning the thought around to *"My mother does love me"* won't work unless I *really feel the truth of those words in my heart*. If I don't, then no change will happen. It is also necessary to keep doing the practice until it finally sinks in. Keeping at it is key here.

The idea that thoughts and feelings are not true in themselves is very different than anything we humans have heretofore been taught. After all, thoughts are what separate us from the lower animals. Observe what the great thinkers all through the ages have accomplished and are still accomplishing to this day. However, If we look closely at how these great minds function, we see that their most effective and creative works come first and foremost from following their intuition, from the heart. The thoughts that are not true are those that flow consistently through our minds at every moment and are either worrisome or negative, or just plain needless for our wellbeing and peace. The real trap comes when we *believe these thoughts* and allow them to bring us down, to affect our relationships, to scare us, to make us lose our *joie de vivre*. As Katie says, *"If a thought troubles you, it's simply not true for you."* And as Jesus once advised: *"Let not your hearts be troubled, nor let them be afraid."* Furthermore, as I was taught years ago, *whatever troubles you does not come from God.*

I see now that when I created such havoc by paying attention to the thought: *"I should examine these negative thoughts,"* I was simply believing a thought that, by the very fact that it was troublesome, was not true for me.

About a year ago, I came across this interpretation from a teacher of *A Course In Miracles* for living in the present moment:

> *"In the Holy Instant, you turn inward, away from the universe of form, and touch God, and you realize that God is what is Real, and the universe of form, and your thoughts about it, are nothing."* (Liz Cronkite, mentor for *A Course in Miracles*). How lovely and how true.

In Glenda Green's book entitled: *Love without End*, which I read a few years ago, Jesus appeared to her and revealed a new way of dealing with life on this plane. At one point she was given a very helpful way of dealing with all the world's pain: Glenda quotes Jesus as saying, *"One can feel sorrow and compassion for others' misfortunes, but it is important not to let oneself be overwhelmed by all the misery of the world. One needs to go within to that place where the Father is, and know that all is well as it is."* Jesus was talking from the Father's perspective which is definitely very different from our own myopic viewpoint and for most people quite difficult to accept. Until we can come to a deep realization of *God's unconditional Love for us* we won't be able to fathom and receive the profound Truth that *"all is well"* for ourselves.

Sometime ago I learned a very powerful way of praying from a book by Gary Renard entitled *The Disappearance of the Universe*. Gary was taught the *prayer of forgiveness* by the beings who came to him to teach him a new way of interpreting Jesus's teachings. The prayer goes like this:

"You are Christ, pure and innocent. All is forgiven. All is released." This prayer has been very instrumental in helping me deal with anger, impatience, and frustration in times of upsets with others and with myself.

About the time that I came across the prayer, we were in the midst of a nor'easter in our part of the world. I watched with trepidation as the big snowplow came down my hill. I had a fragile young tree growing on my front lawn whose tiny branches could easily be broken off by the heavy snow being pushed onto it. I instinctively went out the front door, and at the moment when the plow was stopped and the driver was just about to start pushing the snow towards my tree again, I caught his eye and raised my right hand to stop him. He stopped, but did so very reluctantly; in fact he was furious! I could see him mouthing words as he passed in front of my house that were probably anything but courteous and kind.

Subsequently he took out his frustration on me every time he came to plow. I would hear the plow going back and forth, back and forth, as he went by the house. Sure enough, on looking out, I saw him backing the plow down the hill, picking up as much snow and ice as he could, and dumping it at the end of my driveway on his way up. He did this many times to build as impenetrable a wall of heavy, icy snow as possible. I was totally appalled and shocked that he would get even in such a way. Then the prayer of forgiveness came to mind: *"You are Christ, pure and innocent. All is forgiven. All is released."* I repeated this prayer over and over again as I watched him determinedly, and no doubt, gleefully, do his job. What happened next was a total revelation to me. *I'm* the one who eventually felt released from anger and frustration! I was at peace, and joyful, and felt absolutely no anger or irritation towards him. It was easy to simply forgive the irritated man and send good thoughts and love his way. I use this prayer a lot in my dealings with people and with events in my life, though it is at times hard to do. I need to constantly remind myself that no matter what people say or do, we all have God within and we all need to love one another. Then when I say the prayer, it does its work in me. Indeed, what greater love can I give to myself and to others than to forgive and forgive and forgive *ad infinitum*.

Recently I asked the Father to really know in the depths of my being that I am one with the One. I was having a Reiki session from my friend, Charli, and enjoying a quiet, restful time. Suddenly, this deep, deep, voice came out of my mouth, *"THERE IS NO SEPARATION!"* I felt a change come over me: physically, my face felt different, somehow bigger. I was in such profound peace that it would have been unbearable to come out of that state right then. Charli was aware of what happened, stopped her work for a few minutes, then quietly went on to finish the session. Afterwards, by mutual understanding, neither of us said a word. I couldn't; the need to stay with that intense feeling was too powerful. She respected that, for which I was very grateful. Some time later we talked about it and marveled at the different ways that Spirit works in our lives.

I dwelt on those powerful words and felt their calming effect for several days, pondering the profound Truth that they revealed: *we are not separate from God or from one another.* Just lately I came across the book *The Wisdom Jesus*, by Cynthia Bourgeault in which she writes: "there is no separation between God and humans. When Jesus talks about this Oneness, he is not speaking in an eastern sense about an equivalency of being, *such that I am in and of myself divine.* What he more has in mind is a complete, mutual indwelling: *I am in God, God is in you, you are in God, we are in each other.* There is no separation between humans and God because of this mutual *interabiding* which expresses *the indivisible reality of divine love.* We flow into God—and God into us—because it is the nature of love to flow."

What an awesome and enlightening teaching this is! How different our world would be if we all lived by these words. But we *can* make a difference, now, each of us, by taking these words to heart and making them as real as we can in our lives.

One time I asked a retreat master that I'd been in correspondence with, what answer he could give me to the question, *"Is God nothing?"* His answer was simple and clear, and has been reiterated by many spiritual teachers: *"God is nothing—and everything."* Over the years I've pondered this answer many times but never really understood it. Then a few nights ago, I was listening to one of Adyashanti's talks on YouTube, and he gave an answer that made sense to me. He talked about the two distinctive paths to enlightenment or union with God: 1) *Christian mysticism, which invites us to see everything and everyone as a manifestation and expression of God; and 2) Eastern mysticism, which teaches us that all matter, all form, is nothing, and that God is the Only Reality.* These are two sides of the same coin, and though I'll never completely understand either tradition, it feels right on to me, and so I strive to embrace both teachings in my life.

SOUL MATE, ARE YOU OUT THERE SOMEWHERE?

Along with doing massage work, attending workshops, and spending quality time with friends, every spring I'd get a familiar longing: Is there a soul mate for me out there somewhere? I'd peruse the papers, meet a few hopefuls for lunch, get a conversation going, and give up trying until the following spring.

One year, something really funny happened when I met a very nice man named Francis, uncle to a dear male friend of mine. Francis was beautiful! We hit it off right away. It was summer, and we took strolls through the lovely parks in the area and walked on the warm, sandy beaches. On the third date, walking with arms around our waists, he looked at me and with a gentle smile, asked, "Do you think we could… ?" He didn't have to finish the sentence. "We certainly could," I replied. We went to my house and lovingly embraced. When it was over, I looked at him and in my naivete and innocence said, "That was wonderful! It didn't hurt at all because you're so small." The look of incredulity and total shock on his face hit me like a ton of bricks! He got up, dressed, and left without saying a word. Not surprisingly I never heard from him or saw him again. How was I supposed to know that what I'd said was just not something you told a guy? Needless to say, I never made that blithering mistake again!

A couple of years later, I received a phone call from Emery, a dear friend and client, informing me that she'd sort of fixed me up for a date. I couldn't believe it. "You didn't!" I exclaimed. She'd participated in a workshop that had some kind of spiritual tag attached to it, and there met an older man who was looking for a woman who was interested in spirituality. She said she thought of me right away. He was a nice-looking man, quite a bit older than I was, but seemed very gentle and kind. I argued that this was not the way I wanted to meet somebody. She came back with, "It won't hurt to try, Viv." She went on for quite some time, and my curiosity aroused, I gave in. She was going to give him my phone number, and he'd call. I wondered what I was getting myself into.

Harry turned out to be a nice enough man. He lived some thirty five minutes away, which suited me fine. He came to get a massage every two weeks, and I went to his home on weekends. He wanted to be sexual very early on and I resolutely declined until we'd both been tested for HIV. After all, what did I know about this man? Eventually, I found him to be a good enough lover and it was fun for a while. He wanted to get married; I didn't. He was definitely not someone that I could talk spirituality with. In fact, we had very little in common. The weekends were always the same: arrive at his home, make love, go for lunch at the cheapest place he could find, come back to the house, play cribbage, have something to eat, go to sleep in our own beds (thank God), make love in the morning, have breakfast, and go home. BORING!

I spent a little over two years dating Harry. The fact that my friends loved him and thought he was the "greatest," influenced me in sticking it out. After all, "You gotta give a guy a chance." So I did… until I began noticing a mean streak in him. He had been married three times before, and often enough would accuse me of doing something that was totally off the wall. I realized he was thinking of me as though I were one of his former wives. Finally, he said something that was cruel and nasty and simply wouldn't let go of his absolute righteousness. He went on and on through supper, through a game of cribbage, through the evening, and as I left the next morning. On my way home, I woke up. He expected me to *think* like him. That did it. The following week, I did not call him as I usually did on a Wednesday. I didn't call any other day either. When he called on the Saturday, I could tell by his voice that he knew something was up. I told him I needed a break. Then I asked him to consider going for counseling and said I would be willing to go with him. I said unless he did this, I would not see him again. He didn't say much, but flatly refused to consider counseling. I did not back down.

I was surprised at my reaction. I did not expect to feel any pain around my decision, because I was not that attached to him. It was my first time ever ending a long relationship, and I was experiencing withdrawal. I had planned to go to a drumming gathering in my neighborhood that evening but really didn't feel like going. After sharing with my friend, Gill, that I'd broken up with Harry, and truly preferred staying home, she wisely encouraged me to go to the session, saying that it would probably be very healing for me. So I went and sat down on the floor with the others.

The minute the drums and crystal bowls began playing, I felt all the tension and stress that had built up inside me simply disappear. I felt refreshed, relaxed, and full of wondrous peace and joy. What a blessed two hours I spent taking in the sacred sounds, swirling and spinning and diving, in and out and around me, through me, filling my being to the very core and reverberating throughout the entire room. At the end, filled with the rhythm still beating in the marrow of my bones and in every cell of my body, I went home, went to bed, and slept like a log.

The following Wednesday, Harry came calling. When I answered the door, I was a little shaken to see him. He was red-eyed and unshaven and looked very miserable. He came in with a paper bag holding something I'd left behind. I took it, and he said, "I've changed." I reminded him that one doesn't change that quickly and again asked if he would go for counseling with me. He refused. I stood my ground, said "Goodbye" again, watched him depart with a heavy heart, and never saw him again. His daughter and her husband popped in on me a short time later to try to persuade me to give the relationship another chance, but I simply refused. They left a little dejected, but never bothered me further.

I cannot believe how free I felt after I stopped seeing Harry. The break-up happened at just the right time, for shortly after leaving him, the chance to go to the retreats led by M.C. in the Blue Hills of Virginia opened up, and the liberty to avail myself of the teachings of Eckhart Tolle, Byron Katie, and Adyashanti became possible. I was again able to plunge into the deep waters of solitude and silence needed for an ever-growing relationship with Christ and the Father.

I learned a few lessons from this experience: 1) friends are really well- intentioned, but you don't stay in a relationship because *they like* a guy; 2) if, from the first, a man is not true to what he's portrayed himself to be (for instance, someone looking for a "spiritual" relationship) then you can be pretty sure that he will not always be truthful in other areas of life; 3) also, unless you really don't mind eating on the cheap rather than eating healthily, leave—he's not going to change. There were other lessons to be learned here, but it would be many years before I ventured into another relationship and had the opportunity to deeply look at what I needed to see in myself in order to have a healthy, blossoming partnership, if indeed that was what I really wanted.

WHAT IS THIS ALL ABOUT?

A significant event in my life happened on December 6, 2006. It was a beautiful sunny day in late morning. I had gone to the local market to get a few things. I was dressed warmly, for it was quite cool. As I stepped out of the store I felt something on my left side. I turned, looked up, and saw a truck coming at me! The driver was looking sideways and did not see me. I put my left arm up to stop him, and POW—I went flying through the air! I felt myself *falling gently to the pavement,* which somehow felt as yielding as a thick soft mattress when I landed. I lay there in agony, my whole body shaking in a spasm of horrible pain. All the while I was thinking, *I can't believe this is happening to me.* The driver from the truck came and knelt down beside me, saying over and over, "I'm sorry, I'm sorry, I'm sorry." Wanting to comfort him, I tremblingly and falteringly said, "I understand." How could I not forgive him?

A woman came out of the store and held my head and neck, saying, "I'm a nurse. Stand back." She asked me if my head hurt. I replied that it didn't, saying, "My head and neck are okay. It's my right leg and left arm that are hurting." I had to repeat that several times to the medics when they arrived. Not having experienced the gentle impact that I'd felt upon hitting the ground they did not believe that my neck and head could be fine. Finally, when the morphine was applied, the pain subsided and I stopped shaking. I was transported to the hospital and lay in the Emergency Room waiting for a doctor. I remember noticing my friend, Westy, sitting close by just to be there with me. The morphine made me feel so great that I was telling jokes to one and all. Everything was funny. I joked with the doctor when he showed up after looking at the X-rays and announced that my leg looked bad (punctuated with "very" three times over) and that my wrist was also in bad condition. I didn't care, I didn't have a worry in the world.

I remember the doctor giving me another injection, this one in my left arm to numb it. He then bent and pressed my wrist one way and the other while setting all the little bones in place where they belonged. I could hear the clicking of the bones as he worked on them but, remained calm. I marveled at the fact that it didn't hurt. I liked this doctor! When he finished, he told me that he could do the surgery that my right leg needed but, "because I like you," he said, "I'm going to ask the best in the business to do the surgery." He meant Dr. Matthew, who had worked extensively with wounded soldiers on the battlefields of Iraq.

That evening, I recall sitting up in bed after becoming sick from my supper. The attendant had just left and I felt myself swooning. Before passing out, I pressed the bell at my side. I don't know how long I was out but, at some point I started seeing squares of different colors, reds and blues and greens and yellows—beautiful. Then the colors disappeared as a black bar started coming into my field of vision just below the colors. I heard a gentle voice saying, "Vivian?" I opened my eyes and smiled into the most gorgeous blue eyes I'd ever seen. She looked like an angel, wearing a truly beatific smile as she awakened me. My bed was surrounded by hospital attendants but, to me, they all appeared to be angels looking down on me. I was told later that I had given everybody a real scare in not responding to the voices of nurses calling me. I must say that "other worldly" episode was a very nice way of ending a traumatic day.

There followed a long wait for surgery. My knee was swollen to the size of a watermelon, and the operation would have to wait until the swelling subsided. Thankfully, I had a room to myself and was lovingly and tenderly cared for by nurses and aides at all times of the day and night. It was humiliating to be so helpless and have to get help for everything, from bedpan to washing up. I'll never forget the first time a young, handsome male nurse came to wipe my behind. "It's all right," he said, "We do this all the time!" Strangely, that didn't make me feel any better. I got a kick out of two of the nurses who came around in the middle of the night. They were both white-haired, tall and handsome women, who had a stern appearance but were surprisingly warm-hearted. They'd been school friends who had worked together for years and they joked and laughed while they worked. They were my kind of people and greatly helped lighten up the dreary hospital atmosphere. I missed them when other nurses took their place but, after all, I'd been blessed to have them as my nurses even for a short while.

My friends, God bless them, were right there for me. They visited me daily, the dear ones. They brought me flowers, fruit and most importantly, their loving presence. Healing salves and healing hands were placed on me and brought me great comfort. I was out of it most of the time, as I was kept heavily sedated. At some point I remember remarking to friends Ann and Gill, "Not even the oatmeal tastes good here. How can anybody make a mess out of oatmeal?" For sure, that must have been due to the heavy pain medications.

I slept through most of the long days and was pretty upbeat the times I was awake, but I could take waiting only for so long. My patience was wearing thin. Finally, on the seventh day after the accident, I was wheeled into the surgical area. I remember seeing a very large X-ray of my leg displayed on the wall while the two doctors on the surgical team stood in front of it, frowning. The tibia had been split in two lengthwise and spread wide on either side of the knee, which was also hugely damaged. I inwardly wondered how they would ever fix this mess. They put me under for the surgery. Then, upon awakening some time later, I was pleasantly surprised to see one of my friends sitting by the door smiling at me. I cried out, "Ann!" and went right back to sleep. She'd come a good distance to be with me, and I was extremely grateful. How blessed I am to have such friends.

The surgery was very successful much to everyone's great delight. When the doctor came into my room he exclaimed, "Everything fell right into place!" He was tickled pink with the results, and every time he came to show me additional X-rays, he'd rave about the "excellent" progress I was making. I was not overly impressed as I had not expected anything less, and had never worried about the outcome. I think people were surprised that my seventy-five-year old woman's body could heal so well and so quickly. I was in good health and had taken very good care of myself through the years I'd been on my own. I knew the Father was still looking out for me, but wondered if there was some reason behind the accident. I knew the answer would come sooner or later, I simply needed to be patient.

TO THE NURSING HOME

A week later, I left for a rehab center in a nursing home in Portland. Being in such a facility was both necessary and unbelievably difficult. I had never been inside a place like this, and I could not believe the dimensions of the room I was put in. I had a roommate on the other side of a curtain. There was a chair next to my bed, and a sink in front of the two beds. There was a closet with a toilet facing my bed and that was it. That comprised the length and width of my room. This could be a very depressing experience if I allowed it to be but, I was determined to make the best of it. Resolutely, I practiced the lessons I had learned: specifically, accepting what is, and living in the present moment. This last was quite difficult to achieve since I had not mastered that particular teaching and, in fact, am still working at it.

My neighbor was a dear old lady in her eighties who had a great sense of humor and was an excellent conversationalist. She had one very bad habit though, she needed her television on all the time, day and night, with the sound turned high. I'd ring for the aide at night and would ask him/her to please bring the TV volume down since Gail was sleeping anyway.

Some aides would lower the volume while others would shut the TV off completely. It was a big issue for me and was pretty hard to accept.

On the other hand, as far as Gail was concerned, *I* was a problem for *her*. I had many visitors and telephone calls, and she was very disturbed by all the noise coming from my side of the curtain. Quite a conundrum. There was only one thing to do, which Gail, who was the older and had been there the longest, took upon herself to do. One day some aides came into the room, gathered all her belongings, helped her into a wheelchair, and moved her into another room. She quietly left the premises while smiling apologetically. It was a perfect solution and we promised to visit each other's rooms as she departed.

The staff was overworked but very kind. Live-in conditions left much to be desired but the good people who cared for us helped to lessen the burden of confinement by their genuine concern for our well-being. I was always grateful that no matter what time of day or night, the call-bells were answered as quickly as humanly possible. The staff in rehab was efficient and devoted; they cheered me on at the least sign of progress. Being able to get up by myself to go to the bathroom, was a *huge* accomplishment. I remember the first time I had to *go up* a few steps—it seemed such an insurmountable task! Eventually, with the help of one of the nurses while I held on to the railing, I slowly and laboriously climbed up the stairs, and came back down again. I was beginning to see a light at the end of the tunnel, and felt that I would never take anything for granted again. Every step forward was amazing, marvelous, and new. Life ahead of me was very promising!

It sometimes happened that a nurse or an aide would unintentionally cause pain while working on a patient. One young nurse, fresh from nursing school, who was very devoted and kind, did something that made me cry out in agony, then sob my heart out. I have a high tolerance for pain, but in my weakened condition, with nerves still very raw, I could not help but let my discomfort show. Needless to say, the nurse felt awful, corrected the situation, apologized and left my room shamefacedly. I felt very badly for her; it was not her fault and I did not want her to feel guilty. Not long after I started walking, I had an opportunity to make amends. She was bending over the desk in the hallway, her back to me, and I went behind her, put my arms around her shoulders, and held her. She silently turned to face me, we looked deeply into each other's eyes, and gave each other a warm and loving hug. Not a word was said, but the healing was complete. Every time we came across each other after that, we'd make eye contact and simply smile. How lovely and simple it is to turn a difficult situation into a moment of grace.

Something that touched me very deeply shortly after I'd been in rehab happened early one morning, before breakfast and before I'd washed up. The curtain at the foot of my bed parted and a youngish man came through. Though I'd never seen him, I knew who he was right away, and opened my arms and beckoned him to me. Al was the driver of the truck that had struck me. He'd read the article that had appeared in the pages of a local paper that week, entitled *"Ex-Nun Hit by Truck Feels only Love"* and he said he simply *had* to come and see me. He had a good cry, and so did I. He told me he hadn't slept since the accident and had not yet told his young son and daughter about it. I assured him that I didn't blame him, and wanted more than anything else that he be good to himself and live his life as he did before the accident. I told him there was a reason for things happening the way they did, and some day that would be made very clear to both of us. We didn't talk for very long that day, but we've been friends ever since. Before he left he asked me if there was anything I wanted? I asked, "Could you get me an ice cream bar from Lois' Natural Food Store, please?" He gladly consented, and the next time he visited, we sat contentedly eating our treats. He also told me that he would always be there to help me out with anything I needed done in my house, I simply had to ask him and he would come.

Al has been as good as his word. He has helped me in so many ways without ever charging me. Not only that, but he has become one of my clients. His work is physically demanding, and he greatly benefits from my type of massage work. Our friendship has been one of the many blessings that resulted from this freakish accident.

Al eventually shared with me his viewpoint of what had happened. He told me, "I had stopped the truck to let a lady and her two-year old son pass by on the crosswalk," he explained. "She signaled me to go on *and I didn't see you!* Oh my God! Oh my God! . . ." And we hugged. In due course he was able to forgive himself and live his life on an even keel again. Accidents *can* have happy endings!

I am indebted for life to my wonderful nieces, great nieces, and nephew who came from far and wide to lend me succor and love during my stay in the nursing home. Their caring and thoughtfulness boosted my morale and helped me sail through some very difficult days. It was always such a delightful surprise to see them come through the door with their warm smiles and hugs. They brought me so much joy! I am also deeply grateful to my many wonderful friends who brought me healthy and nutritious foods throughout my time there, and who provided alternative healing to my aching body as often as they could. Blessings on all of you!

It doesn't surprise me that I found it hard to pray during my time at the nursing home. What with the pain meds I was taking and the general overall weariness and weakness that I felt, I was not really at my best. But I do remember telling God as I was leaving rehab, "Lord, I've done my stint in a nursing home, and *this is it! I never want to go through this again.*" I think He heard me.

After about seven weeks in the nursing home, I was allowed to return to my own home, to be greeted by my two beloved cats, Coney and Mickey, and by caring neighbors who were ready to do all they could to help me readjust and get settled.

My dear friends, Gill and Charli, had done an incredible job of cleaning up my house before I returned, so I walked into a home that was sparkling and cheery and full of light. How wonderful! One thing was amiss though; even with the help of a walker, I still could not get up the two high steps to the door by myself. My sweet friend, Allan, who, besides being a great massage therapist and gardener, is also an excellent builder, went to work right away and rebuilt my little porch, adding an extra step to make things easier for me. Allan would never accept payment for his labor. He is such an angel.

I could not shower without help, or cook, or take care of my cats' needs, or do any housework at all for a while. A cherished friend, Sarah, (now at Home with God, dear heart) contacted one of her friends who helped people like me, and soon Rosie showed up. She was a wonderful, jovial and caring person; just what I needed. With her help I improved quickly, and soon she didn't need to stay overnight. A visiting nurse also came around for a few weeks, to supervise my exercises and to give me additional workouts to further my recovery. I had all the help I needed.

It would be some time before I could drive, as my right leg was still healing but again, friends lovingly chauffeured me around to do errands. What an amazing support system I had. I am one lucky gal! At some point in time, I suddenly realized that God/Presence/Source kept coming through for me as He'd always done, by means of my friends. I had never been alone… He had always been there for me.

THE MOST BENEVOLENT OUTCOME

The very next day after the accident, one of my friends wisely advised me to get a lawyer. Thankfully, one of my clients, a psychologist, is married to a lawyer whom I knew and trusted implicitly. He is a good man, but mainly a divorce lawyer, and when I spoke with him, he assured me that his partner, Reggie, would be the ideal person to take on a case like mine. I thanked God for his guidance and gladly accepted his proposition. I did not meet Reggie until I was in the nursing home, where he came to inform me about the details of the procedure. I had absolutely no idea how much paper work and how many phone calls back and forth were involved in order to get the best deal possible for me. This could be a very long process indeed, depending on the company that carried Al's insurance.

As I soon found out, his insurance company was one of the most difficult companies Reggie had ever worked with. The company would use delaying tactics to prolong the case as much as possible, until going to court was the only alternative.

This we did not want to do. So Reggie started early on to negotiate with them, spurring them on to get going with this case and come up with a settlement that would be acceptable to him and his client, the former nun. Yes! He used my prior status remorselessly. This was, according to him, a good and acceptable strategy. One of the first things he did was send a copy of the newspaper article that had been written about the accident, *"Ex-Nun... Feels Only Love."* That, apparently, impressed the woman in charge of negotiations very favorably.

After I had the initial meeting with Reggie, he'd arranged for me to have a phone session with the negotiator. I answered the negotiatior's questions as best as I could. I was still pretty weak, and my voice trembled a little, but I spoke truthfully of what had happened. Reggie had warned me not to tell her that Al and I had become friends, since that would work against me. After the phone call was over, I asked Reggie how I'd made out. He said, "On a scale of one to ten? Ten!" That felt really good.

I was contacted again and again, and asked the same questions over and over. It seems that's a tactic that is generally used in order to see if people stick to the same story or deviate at all from the original narration. My answers were always perfectly clear, and I never digressed through exaggeration or otherwise. I just patiently and slowly spelled out, again and again, what had happened. I never lost my cool or got angry or annoyed at them, even though I sometimes felt like saying, "I've answered this a dozen times. Don't you get it?" Instead I stayed calm and collected, breathing deeply in order to remain that way.

Reggie was getting nervous about getting a settlement and finally decided to set a date for the company to come to a decision. Either they settled by this certain date, or we'd go to court, a prospect I did not want to even think about. This went on for the whole time I was at the nursing home, and by the time I got back home, (almost two months after the accident), nothing had yet been resolved. The date set for getting a final answer was getting closer, and Reggie was putting more pressure on the company. The agent he always spoke with reassured him that the company was definitely working on the case, and it would soon come to a resolution.

In the meantime I called Sue Yarmey, a friend, who is a psychic and tarot card reader. During the reading she gave me, she said that I was going to come into some money. She asked me if I was in a relationship? I replied negatively, and filled her in on our efforts to get a good settlement from the insurance company. She then suggested that I use the mantra MBO or *"Most Benevolent Outcome"*[1] when asking for a good compensation, leaving the upshot to God. This seemed like a great approach to me. And so for the next two weeks I repeated those words many times a day as I thought of the deliberations going on.

At the end of the two weeks Reggie phoned me. The Universe had come through sooner than anticipated. We had received a settlement beyond his highest expectations! I thanked him and smilingly told him about the MBO mantra I'd been using for the previous two weeks. He then called the adjustor and passed this information on to him. About twenty minutes later Reggie called and excitedly told me that the insurance company had unhesitatingly upped the settlement by another *twenty thousand dollars*. Reggie and his partner had never experienced anything like this, especially from *this* company. They were ecstatic! They kept saying I had a direct line to God. "Maybe" I replied," but don't we all?"

When I went to their office a few weeks later to sign papers and pick up the check, there were hugs and exclamations of joy all around. I thanked them profusely for the excellent work they'd done, and suggested they use the MBO mantra regularly to help other clients. "We're not about to do that," they said.

"It probably wouldn't work for anybody else but you." Too bad they felt that way. It cannot do any harm, and may very well do a whole lot of good.

WHAT... AGAIN??

Amidst all the healing that was happening, something was going on with my leg. On my last visit of the year with Dr. Matthew, I told him I wanted the metal plate, pins and screws removed from my leg because they were digging into my shin and causing a lot of discomfort. He was okay with doing that, and we set up a time for another surgery. While the leg was opened up, another doctor cleaned out the debris around the knee which had accumulated since the first surgery. With the pins and screws and metal plate removed, I felt I was going to be fine, no more leg problems.

Alas! I was wrong. A year or so later, I returned to see my surgeon, and showed him what was going on: the leg was leaning to the right from the knee down. I was walking crooked and with increasing difficulty. He then referred me to another doctor for tests and X-rays, because he only repaired broken bones, nothing else, he said.

This new doctor, one of the best in his field, was Dr. Matthew's exact opposite as far as bedside manners were concerned. In short, he had none, but he was an excellent surgeon, and that's all that mattered. After X-rays were taken and he showed me the films, I was appalled at what I saw. He smiled and remarked, "You see it, don't you." The entire leg was going east. He offered several options other than a knee replacement, but I chose the latter route rather than a process that would require my going for check-ups every year. That was not the way I wanted to go.

The surgery went well, but this is the kind of surgery where the recovery is much harder and more painful than the operation. It can take months before one can walk without a limp and without a cane. Some folks never recover completely because they can't take the pain of being on a machine that stretches all the muscles and fibers and ligaments as much as one can endure, five to six hours a day. I started bending my knee at 90 degrees while still in the hospital, and upon my return home went up one agonizing notch at a time; each additional stretch as bad as when I first started. I moaned and groaned a lot during the three or four weeks of this process, and was simply overjoyed when I finally reached my goal of bending my knee to 120 degrees. My only prayer had been one of simply accepting the pain—"It's OK, it's all right, it is what it is," and my greatest comfort had come from the support of family and friends who cheered me on to the very end.

At the time of the surgery, a dear nephew of mine, Michael, with whom I'd recently reconnected, offered to come and stay with me for a whole month! I was really touched by his generosity and kindness. It was so wonderful to get to know this great gentle giant of a man. He helped make my life much easier, and the pain much less, by helping me out in every way he could and simply being there for me. During his time with me, Michael, at the cost of much pain from his chronic back issues, built a shelf to go under my picture window: an ideal place for my plants. Our friendship has kept blossoming through these years, even though he lives miles away in Bangor, Maine. I am eternally grateful to him for bringing so much sweetness and love into my life.

When I finally walked with just a cane for support, I couldn't contain my pride: I'd done it! It had taken weeks of excruciating pain, but it was all worth it, and the pain was quickly forgotten in the delight of being able to walk up and down the hills where I live. That, along with other required exercises and stretches, worked wonders for me. No one would ever guess that my leg had ever been so damaged. I also had the perfect remedy for recurring pain: wrapping my leg in an ice cold gel-pack. Nothing helped me as much. No pain-killers for me.

When I went to the surgeon's office for my final check-up, he was so impressed by my flexibility and mobility that he said, "See you in two years." Two years went by and I never got a call from his office to come in for a check-up. I didn't see the need to remind him, so I didn't, and haven't to this day, five years later.

SOUL MATES GALORE!

At some point, I once again started looking for a soul mate. I'd met a couple of men through the internet in the years after my one long-term relationship of a little over two years, but none of them met my criteria. I was pretty fussy and, I think, with good reason. Then a little over four years ago, I met someone who was good, kind, courteous, generous, and a real gentleman. We saw each other for a while and had some good times. However, after all these years, I discovered something about myself that I had not realized before: I am very happy loving everybody. I am not happy in an exclusive relationship. My friend was extremely considerate, but his constant attention became too much for me. I felt boxed in, and finally understood that probably no relationship would give me the same freedom as being on my own. For me, real love has to go beyond just being a physical attraction or interaction with one person, especially as I get older. I need to have space for other people to love and do things with. I love my life and am quite content to live by myself.

Just lately I have come to appreciate that I have many soul mates. I believe that there are different levels of being a soul mate. A few people that I share with are pretty much at the same place where I am on the spiritual path; they are the ones that I can share with at a deep level; other friends are soul mates because of the love, companionship and good times we have together. Still others I feel a kinship with because they've been devoted friends for years, and we have a mutual love and respect for each other. I also feel a deep bond with my clients, the present ones and those I had in past years. I care deeply for the lovely, beautiful people I am a companion to in the nursing homes that I visit weekly, as well as the devoted folks who are my co-workers in hospice. I feel close to the wonderful people I've bartered with in my line of work, as well as those who have ministered to me with their own healing modalities. I consider the many members of my family of several generations (I have been an aunt, great-aunt, and great-great-aunt for many years) soul mates in a very special way; the family ties have deepened with the passing of time, which gives me much joy. These are my soul mates, one and all, and I am blessed beyond belief to be part of their lives.

GOD'S PRECIOUS ONES

I have mentioned some of the blessings that resulted from the accident: my relationship with Al, which has continued through almost eight years; getting a good settlement from his insurance company which provides me with some security for the time I have left in this world; and lastly, getting a good push towards what I consider to be my third calling: volunteering in a nursing home. I had thought of doing this work for years, but I'd always found an excuse not to follow through.

A year or so after the accident, I felt it was high time I paid attention to this inner voice and did something about it. One day one of my friends told me that a training program for volunteers was soon to take place in an organization called Beacon Hospice. I contacted the volunteer coordinator, Donna Teague, who spelled out what the work would entail, and cordially invited me to take the training. I signed up and started the required seven-week-long program along with a few other interested persons, both male and female.

Surprisingly this work has turned out to be another of those life-changing experiences; I would never have thought that this labor of love would mean so much to me. To my surprise and delight, it has become an incredibly uplifting and satisfying task. I get so much more from the dear people I visit than I can ever give them.

I soon discovered that I really enjoyed working with patients with dementia or Alzheimer's. I shared this with my coordinator, who was very pleased because this could be a solution to a problem she was having. Most volunteers, for some reason or other, do not want to work with people who have this illness, so she had difficulty finding someone willing to visit them.

I have only wonderful stories to tell about my work with dementia patients. One thing that I soon realized was that they, like small children, are very wary of me when they first see me. But mostly, all I need do is come as close as is comfortable for them, look into their eyes, and smile. It may take a few visits for some of them to feel at ease with me and let me in, but there's never been a time when the bonding has not happened sooner or later; then we simply take it from there.

Some of the patients who were in the early stages of dementia were still quite articulate. One little patient, Lucy, always gave me the brightest smile, eyes glowing all the while, and would come out with really quite apt responses to people and situations. One time a worker in maintenance with whom I'd had some conversations, stopped by when Lucy and I were visiting, and started talking about some difficulty in her work situation. She went on and on about it, obviously needing someone to listen to her. When she left, Lucy, who'd been listening intently, looked up at me and said, with a great big grin on her face, "She's got a problem, doesn't she!" She was so right on about that. I'd say that's pretty good awareness for a person with dementia.

Sadly I saw Lucy's condition gradually worsen. She'd had Parkinson's for a long time; her limbs were getting more and more rigid, and her speech was so soft that I could hardly make out what she was saying. Even as the disease progressed, though, Lucy did not lose her smile or her sense of humor. She was very observant of peoples' behavior and mannerisms, and got a kick out of all that went on around her. She didn't miss a thing, and she'd see the humor behind the human drama. It got harder and harder for me to understand her, but it was evident that she enjoyed life and was not afraid of dying. When I spoke to her of the joy and peace and love that was awaiting her on the other side, she couldn't speak anymore but she didn't have to. She lit up, her face and her eyes saying it all. She was looking forward to moving on to her heavenly home. I couldn't be by her side when her time came and I was sorry about that, but I did send my love to be with her as she made her peaceful transition into the Light.

Whenever I visit the nursing home, I always give some attention to the dear people sitting around. One sweet looking little lady always sat by herself and never made eye contact with anybody. I noticed her because she seemed to be so alone. When I walked by her, she always looked the other way, so I made no effort to approach her. Then one day, my hospice coordinator told me there was a patient who'd been accepted into the hospice program weeks before, but no one could make any headway with her. Would I be willing to take her on? "Sure," I said, "I'll be glad to try." At my next visit to the Home, I went looking for my new patient and was pleasantly surprised to find out that she was none other than the dear little loner I'd been interested in meeting.

At my first visit with Peg, I sat in front of her, leaving some space between us, and gently greeted her. I told her my name, and said that I'd be visiting her every week. No response. There was a tray attached to her chair and she was sipping juice from a glass which she held with both hands. She was almost finished with her drink but was taking her time savoring every drop. As she slowly sipped, I quietly moved my chair closer and closer. I said a few words, looking directly at her. She, however, never looked at me and kept on sipping. Finally, when there was not one single drop left, she put the glass down. I touched her arm gently, and said, "I love you, Peg." The most amazing thing happened! She looked directly at me, and with a big smile on her beautiful face, gently started rubbing my face: first one side, then the other, up to my forehead and down to my chin, then all around. I slowly bent my head over her lap, and she rubbed the top of my head, all the while smiling lovingly at me. Not a word was said during this entire time, and I remember wondering what she was doing. It felt wonderful and somehow very appropriate. I learned later from one of the aides that she had a great love for horses and used to ride one. And I realized, that's what she was doing: rubbing her horse's neck and head! How absolutely touching. I didn't mind at all being a horse for her.

Every time I visited Peg, we would go through the same ritual, a very satisfying exercise for us both. Conversation was unnecessary. Communication went on at a very deep level where words were not important or needed. She knew all about silence being the great communicator.

Peg passed over in the middle of the night not long after I'd started visiting her. Though I was sorry to hear that she'd gone, I was so happy to have had the opportunity to know her even for that very short period of time. She was one beautiful person, and I'm sure she was greeted by many of her big gentle friends with great love and joy as she went through to the other side.

Working in hospice and with dementia patients has been such an eye-opener for me. I've become aware of the many diverse ways that individuals who seem to have nothing to give, turn out to be the wisest teachers. They, for the most part, have had to learn to receive in all ways, and to do so gracefully and gratefully; something that we, who are healthy, often have difficulty doing. I am thankful for the challenge this work has given me to broaden my horizons and to grow into a deeper love than I ever knew I was capable of.

I stopped going to the nursing home this past winter, 2013-2014: a winter to remember! The traveling was simply too difficult for me; and frankly, I have to admit that driving is not my cup o' tea anymore. I miss my dear old people, but I send them love and light whenever I think of them, and know they are in the loving heart of God. What better place to be?

PART FOUR

LOVE ALONE IS REAL

*"For the mountains may depart, the hills be shaken,
but my Love for you will never leave you…"*
(Isaiah 54: v. 10)

A WAKE-UP CALL

It took another accident to precipitate my getting a reading from my long-time astrologer friend, Alice Hayden. It was in the month of September of 2012 that this totally bizarre and unwarranted accident occurred. I was going out to do some errands, reached for my door, started to open it, and, without having time to even put my hand around the doorknob, suddenly felt as though I'd been lifted off my feet (which were clad in heavy rubber sandals; I was also standing on a rubber-backed rug) and thrown head-first on my back down the flight of stairs to the basement cement floor. It happened so quickly that all I could manage was a few grunts as my spine violently and painfully bumped and thumped down every one of those eight steps. The thought of smashing the back of my head onto the cement floor entered my consciousness and horrified me, but there was nothing I could do to stop the descent. *Miraculously, at the very last moment, some benign energy gently turned me over so that my forehead and knees hit the concrete floor, rather than the back of my head and neck, and I was saved from catastrophic injury.*

I lay on the steps shaken and stunned, hoping I could move my right leg since it had taken the brunt of the fall and was vulnerable from the time the knee had been shattered and subsequently replaced. A stillness came over me, and I asked God, *"What do I do about this?"* I waited for an answer, and suddenly the words of the prayer of forgiveness from the book *The Disappearance of the Universe* came to mind: *"You are Christ, Pure and Innocent; All is forgiven, All is released."* I repeated these words a few times, forgiving the energy that had caused this to happen, and forgiving myself for whatever part I had played in it. Then peace and calm filled me. Slowly and deliberately I moved my leg, and to my great relief and surprise I was able to bend it without difficulty. Nothing was broken, thank God! My next thought was *Ice!* I've got to get to my ice-packs! Carefully, I went up the stairs one step at a time, holding on to the railing, and finally made it to the refrigerator. At last I settled into my recliner holding an ice-pack to my forehead, an ice-pack wound around each knee, and proceeded to call a couple of my friends.

My dear pal, Westy, soon came in and with great sympathy prepared some soup for me to eat when I could. Then, around six o'clock, another friend, Julienne, a homeopathic practitioner whom I'd also called, arrived with a very potent medicine, a strong dosage of arnica, to place under my tongue. Julienne is a farmer and was in the process of seeing to her animals' needs when I called. She said that she sensed the urgency of the situation and felt an energy pushing her to hurry up and come to my aid: *"Go to Vivian, go to Vivian!"* Because of my age and the type of fall I'd sustained, she said, it was crucial that I get help as soon as possible. Sure enough, a half hour after taking the very effective supplement, my head, which had seemed to be twice its normal size, felt about fifty percent better, and Julienne left me with enough arnica to use during the night as needed.

I woke up after ten hours sleep (broken up every two hours) still feeling fuzzy and stiff, but surprisingly without any pain or black and blue marks, except on my forehead and knees and on my left shoulder. I had no serious damage whatsoever. *Amazing!* As somebody has remarked, I am very lucky in my misfortunes; very true, indeed. I took it easy for a few days, then, within a week of the accident, was able to get back to walking my hills and doing my regular chores and activities.

When I went to see Alice a few days later and told her of the episode, she said that being turned over at the very last instant, thus avoiding serious injury, occurred because in that moment I was in another dimension and very well protected. She went on to say that everything in this dimension is going through tremendous upheaval at this time, and that my bumping down the stairs was the Universe's way of getting me to do some interior work that I wasn't aware I needed to do. I'm not sure I fully buy this explanation; but I do believe that all trials come in order to provide us with an opportunity to step back, take stock of our lives and see what changes we need to make. And this, I was willing to do.

A few nights later, I was awakened from a deep and peaceful sleep by my kitty, Elmer, jumping on the bed, and by a very tall woman dressed in a long white robe, standing by the bed. Her right arm was raised high as she suddenly yelled, "IT'S TIME TO WAKE UP!" I became angry, resenting that I'd been so rudely jolted out of blissful, dreamless slumber by this stupid woman! Who or what was she? An angel? A being from another dimension? I had no idea. But the message sounded real enough that it jolted me out of my complacency and I started asking questions.

What was this wake-up call about? What did I need to look at? I knew that I was not to dig into my subconscious mind in order to work out unresolved issues, but rather allow things to come up from the quiet still place within. Sure enough, information soon started to emerge.

One big issue that I hadn't really dealt with was ang*er*. I'd always been averse to admitting that I still had some deep-seated anger within me. As a child and teenager, I repressed my anger so fiercely that I would simply not allow it to come up at all. I thus deluded myself into believing that I was *never* angry. As a nun, anger could show up as my strong dedication to some cause that I would become zealously passionate about and try to share with the Sisters. My efforts at persuasion would invariably get a response that would blindside me. *"What are you so angry about?"* the Sisters would ask, and I would hotly answer, *"I'm not angry!"* I would get deeply frustrated, impatient, irritated and upset about the flagrant injustice in the world, but I would never call those deep feelings anger. That was simply *not me*.

It is just lately that I have come to accept that I've been angry for a very long time. It was Alice's perception about what I shared concerning my oldest sister's anger that opened my eyes: I had found her anger so frightening and ugly that I had promised myself I would *never* be angry like her! And there it is: even though I thought I did not let Velma's angry words in, I was actually being indoctrinated those many times that I listened to her while we were walking. My fury was masked under the guise of arguing against anything that I perceived as wrong. I was essentially feeling deep resentment towards the injustice in the world, which I felt powerless to change.

I still have to learn to accept that I can't help feeling angry at times. The trick is to *acknowledge* the annoyance and *welcome it,* as Cynthia Bourgeault says: *Stay present with the sensation* in your body, then, no matter what the feeling is, welcome it: *"Welcome anger, Welcome fear, Welcome worry, Welcome pain,*

Welcome thoughts," repeating the words over and over until you feel the resistance melt away and the body relax. Then let go with the words: *"I let go of the anger, of the pain, of the fear, of the worry…"* and so on.

I have been pleasantly surprised at how quickly any pain that I experience diminishes as soon as I repeat the words *"welcome pain."* The same can be said for any sensation that I am currently feeling and want to let go.

Letting go of the feeling happens *in the moment.* It doesn't mean I will never become angry, or fearful, or impatient again. But every time I acknowledge a feeling, welcome it, then let it go, it lessens its grasp on my being.

C. Bourgeault quotes Mary Mrozowski, the actual founder of the Welcoming method as preferring the following litany:

> *I let go of my desire for security and survival.*
> *I let go my desire for esteem and affection.*
> *I let go my desire for power and control.*
> *I let go my desire to change the situation.*

Mary actually says that she is thus sending a strong message to the unconscious. The goal is simply to stay present at this deeper level for as long as one can. Quite an agenda, but possible to achieve if one feels called to do the practice.

Subsequently I sustained two other weird falls after being pushed down the stairs. The second fall happened about eight months after the first; the third fall occurred some five months after that. Both falls happened in the house and were totally bizarre and inexplicable. In both instances, saying the *prayer of forgiveness* gave me some much needed relief. After the third occurrence, however, some of my friends suggested that I ask Charli Griffin, my friend and Reiki master, to do a house clearing for me.

This basically involved getting in touch with any negative energy that had taken residence and asking some powerful Archangels (Michael, Raphael, Gabriel and Uriel) to help heal the entities and send them on their way. Indeed, this is what happened. Charli called in the Archangels and they found there were two negative energies in the house: a father and a daughter. They were full of hatred (not directed at me) and were looking for peace. Since mine is a peaceful home and I am a peaceful person, that may be why they chose to come to my house and jolt me until I took action and asked for help, for myself, and for them. Thank God the beings finally left peacefully and joyfully. And many thanks to Charli and to the very powerful Archangels who came to my rescue. Charli suggested that I ask Archangel Michael to surround my house with blue light for protection, which I am very happy to do as often as I think of it. It's good to have him around.

Through all these experiences I have come to realize that *dark energies don't have any real power over us if we forgive them*, and I feel that one of my tasks is to use this prayer as one way of loving everyone and everything and thus help bring about healing to myself, to those I love, and to the whole world. This means forgiving people who use power to control, dominate, and belittle others; forgiving politicians who don't see beyond their need to keep their legislative seats and so neglect the dire needs of their fellow citizens; forgiving those who preach hatred and violence in the name of religion; forgiving the leaders of the Church for distorting the teachings of the gentle Christ with their misguided need for authoritarianism; forgiving the Supreme Court for a decision that has set women's rights back decades; and hardest of all, forgiving myself for the times I have not trusted my own inner wisdom.

We are in a time of unprecedented upheaval, as we witness on a daily basis, but also in a period of possible great transformation, both on an individual and a global level, as amazing as that sounds. Jesus the Christ, who said *"You are the light of the world,"* is asking us to let our light shine on one and all as we allow the Spirit to lead us. We are also asked by Jesus to *"Love your neighbor as yourself."* By this he means: *see your neighbor as a continuation of you . . . not as a separate individual.* Love *them* and you love *yourself!* What a challenge this is, and what a difference it would make in our lives and in our world if we actually saw ourselves in every person and really put Jesus's words into practice. We know we can't do it alone! But we are *never* alone! For Jesus also said *"I am with you till the end of time."*

Thanks be to God, I now recognize that we simply *cannot be separated from God.* It's an impossibility! If that were not the case, we would cease to exist, period. What a lovely and freeing Truth to recognize*: God is <u>always</u> with us* even though *we are often too blinded by our thoughts to be aware of His Presence in our lives.*

ABIDE IN MY LOVE

"*As the Father has loved me, so do I love you. Abide in my love.*" (John: 15; 8-9) For many people, it is impossible to believe in God's unconditional love: "If God loves me, why am I going through all this pain? What about all the suffering that is the lot of most people on this earth? What of all the cruelty and bigotry, greed and misuse of power? How can you say that *God is love?* I don't buy it!"

True, there is a lot of suffering in this world; no one escapes it. What we *do* with the pain and suffering, though, makes all the difference. Some choose to become embittered and angry and stay focused on their misery, thereby increasing their distress. Others choose to *consciously accept* their suffering, and in so doing allow divine light to shine through in their lives. The pain is still there, and they alleviate it as much as possible, but keeping their faith in God's love for them no matter what, somehow helps them keep their joy, peace, and love alive and strong; and so they remain free from bitterness.

Jesus the Christ experienced suffering on a grand scale! But through all the darkness and horrific pain, he *never reneged on love*. In the garden, he prayed "*Not my will but thine be done."* On the cross he cried *"Why have you forsaken me?"* Then, *"Father, forgive them for they know not what they do."* And, *"Father, into your hands I commend my spirit."* He never lost his trust and belief in the Father's love, and went through his agony not to be a sacrifice to pacify a wrathful God, as the church would later express it, but out of *sheer unadulterated love for us*. "Jesus, the lover, willingly lays down his life for the *beloved, humankind*. He loved us all the way to the end." (C. Bourgeault)

A few years ago, when I first read the book *Love Without End* by Glenda Greene, I opened it at random, and the words that Jesus said to the author, *"Glenda, Love is Who You Are," jumped out at me and went straight to my heart*. It felt like He was speaking to *me,* and I knew the Truth of those words and my heart melted in tears of gratitude. But what does it mean to *be love?* Well, if I am part of God, and God is love, I have to ask how am I to *be* love like God?

I believe I am called to *be love* by *emptying myself and dying to myself* as Jesus did. I've always been attracted to this particular teaching of his: *Unless the grain of wheat falls into the ground and dies, it shall not bear fruit.* So how do I die to myself?

Every time I choose to let go of a negative thought either about myself or somebody else and choose to listen to the voice within, *I die a little and grow in love.*

Every time I let go of the past or the future and choose to stay in the present, *I die to myself and love increases*. Every time I choose to help someone, *I die a little and love expands.*

Every time I refrain from judging, from blaming, from being self-righteous and unforgiving, *I empty myself and love takes over*. Every time I acknowledge fear, let it go, and choose to go through fear into love, *I die to myself and love flourishes.*

Every time I accept people where they are and refrain from trying to change them, *I die to myself and love shines brightly*!

I have so many opportunities to empty myself and *allow God to fill me and love through me! This is how I can be love.*

More than ever I believe that people today need to *deeply know that they are loved just as they are, without condition, unreservedly, forever and forever.* All they have to do is to *accept* God's undying love. Then watch the miracles happen.

WHERE AM I NOW?

Gregg Braden in his book *The Spontaneous Healing of Belief* makes it very clear that we can change the belief patterns that have been handed down to us by exploring our core beliefs and letting go of the ones that prevent us from being true to ourselves. From him I have learned that to replace an old belief with a new one, it has to come from the *heart*. If I'm saying an affirmation, for instance, *and I don't feel the joy of it happening in my heart right now, it won't happen*. We can choose how we feel, so it isn't that hard to feel joy, or peace, or love, if we really want to.

And what was the core belief that I lived by for so many years? For a long time I did not trust my intuition and did not believe I had *any* power over my life at all. Even though I was making life-changing choices very early on, I didn't see that I was actually making big decisions on my own. Dear friends had to point that out to me! But gradually throughout the years, I increasingly and consciously followed the urgings of my heart in my search for a life that was acceptable to me, and acceptable to the Father within. And then, when the time came, *I catapulted from years of security and sanctuary* into a world that I'd never experienced before, without ever looking back. And I realized that by the grace of God, I am indeed, a pretty powerful person.

Another core belief that has come to the surface in writing my story, is the one that I accepted as true when I was very young: the belief that there was *something wrong with me.* Simply seeing this for the fiction that it is, has released me from any vestige of the false assumption that had been keeping me from acknowledging myself as *well and healthy and <u>whole</u>.* Thanks be to God for new insights and teachings.

Still, I ask myself, am I really where I want to be? Am I all done with my interior work? *Heavens, no*! I often find myself faced with the same issues I was working on at the beginning of my journey, though at an ever higher level on the spiritual spiral staircase. Therefore I continue to focus on:

Living more consistently in the ever-present moment, which will enable me to live in the Presence at all times. Be the love that I am, which entails self-emptying and dying-to-self so that the Father's love can shine through me. Keep on listening to the Stillness within rather than to the chattering mind. Allow my own direct knowingness of Jesus's undying, all-embracing Love for me be the always accessible gateway to my own inner authority... For starters.

I have just lately become aware of something that's been lacking in my meditation practice. For many years I went to my center within by saying the word "Father," thus quickly coming into deep and profound peace. But when thoughts started to arise, I would too easily and hastily give up the meditation period to go back to my everyday world. Now I realize that intrusive thoughts are simply an *opportunity to return to the Father by letting thoughts go as soon as they arise and as often as they arise.* This quickly brings me back into stillness and deep meditation for awhile. Then, as soon as I notice thoughts returning, I simply let go, and start over... as many times as it takes.

Finally, these words from the Protestant theologian Martin Buber have always fed me on my journey, and are as valid today as they've ever been:

> *The Kingdom of God is the Kingdom of Danger and of Risk;*
> *Of Eternal Beginning and Eternal Becoming;*
> *Of Open Spirit and Deep Realization;*
> *The Kingdom of Holy Insecurity.*[2]

Insecurity can be a catalyst for *seeking security in God*, the only *real Security*. So it's not necessarily a bad thing; simply very challenging. It can also be very empowering depending on what we do with it: fight against it; feel gloomy and downcast because of it; or use it as a tool, and trust that the powerful Love of God will sustain us, never lead us astray, and *never let us down*. Hallelujah!

GOD IS RIGHT HERE RIGHT NOW
I love this moment of Now This eternal Now
When Breath is alive and performs
Its Miracle of Life Pulsing
In Perfect Rhythm
In Wondrous Alignment
With Source Breathing Itself

ENDNOTES

1. www.TheGentleWayBook.com
2. Martin Buber, *Daniel: Dialogues on Realization,* trans. Maurice Friedman (New York: Holt, Rinehart, Winston), 1964(1913), 95

www.ingramcontent.com/pod-product-compliance
Lightning Source LLC
LaVergne TN
LVHW041911070526
838199LV00051BA/2575